ENTERTAI
THE VIRGIN
GUIDE

Also published by Virgin Books:

Buying a Home: The Virgin Guide
Dating: The Virgin Guide
Money: The Virgin Guide

ENTERTAINING: THE VIRGIN GUIDE

Eleni Kyriacou

First published in Great Britain in 2003 by
Virgin Books Ltd
Thames Wharf Studios
Rainville Road
London
W6 9HA

A catalogue record for this book is available from the British Library.

ISBN 0 7535 0749 8

Typeset by Phoenix Photosetting, Chatham, Kent
Printed and bound in Great Britain by Mackays of Chatham, Kent

CONTENTS

This book is dedicated to my mum, Elpida Kyriacou – a great host, a fantastic cook and a truly inspiring woman. And also to Andrew, whose love and unfailing support are as deeply appreciated as are his perfect Kir Royales.

INTRODUCTION

Successful entertaining is not rocket science. Anyone can do it. To be a great host you don't need to be a wonderful cook, have a big house or a fat wallet. You *do* need to understand your guests, know your limits and focus on the kind of event you want to hold. And it goes without saying that the more organised you are, the smoother the ride for you and your guests.

You can also be a perfect host without being a martyr. This book is full of ideas that show how to use shortcuts to save yourself time and make life easy when entertaining. There are also tips from leading experts in the field and a list of resources available to you. The aim is to save you time and effort and help you throw the kind of parties that will be remembered – for all the right reasons. A Sunday lunch for the whole clan shouldn't find you peeling potatoes at 5 a.m. It really is possible to pull it off and still have a lie-in. Although this book does, at times, look at modern manners (or etiquette, as it used to be known), the emphasis is placed firmly on having a good time. The assumption I've made is that most of your events will be informal affairs. Entertaining has become much more relaxed in recent years, and there really are no strict 'rules' to follow. Another title for this book could have been *How to Show your Friends a Good Time (Without Giving Yourself a Breakdown)*.

HOW TO USE THIS BOOK

Part One looks at getting to grips with the basics – who to invite, how, budgeting, food, drink, music, decor and so on. In an ideal world you'd read these chapters in succession as they have a logical sequence that relates to planning your event. In reality, you'll probably want to dip in and out, choosing the areas in which you feel you need more ideas or advice. They can, of course, be read in isolation, hence a certain amount of repetition; if you're in a rush, you can still get a good grasp of the subject, quickly. And for more in-depth detail, I refer you to other chapters as and when needed.

A couple of points of caution – it's *vital* to decide what kind of party you're having at the outset (Chapter 1) and to consider your budget (Chapter 3). Many of your other decisions will stem from these two areas, and it will save you time, money and hassle if you tackle these first. Each chapter in Part One ends with a five-minute checklist (a summary for those in a real rush) as well as mistakes to avoid.

Part Two puts it all into practice by examining specific events in greater detail. It looks at everything from planning a picnic to a wedding reception, with checklists of all the things you need to consider. There are also a few simple recipe ideas thrown in along the way.

And in case you hadn't noticed by now, this *isn't* a guide to protocol or society manners. If you're the kind of person who cares which way to pass the port round the dinner table, I'm afraid you're on your own. If, however, like me, you only care if there's some port left by the time it gets to you, read on!

PART ONE: GETTING TO GRIPS WITH THE BASICS

1 WHAT KIND OF EVENT AND WHY?

You're going to throw a party! Fantastic. You're going to open your home to friends, maybe even family, and your generosity, sociability and sheer wit will be talked about for years. It will, of course, be the best party held. Ever.

Before you go out and start buying family-sized packs of peanuts, dozens of bottles of drink and start inviting everyone you've ever met, stop. Breathe. It's very easy to get carried away once you've decided to plan an event, but these early stages are the crucial ones. It may sound obvious, but the first thing you need to think about is what kind of event you want to plan and who's coming. If you get this straight, the rest will come a lot easier.

It's much easier, for example, to decide on what the invitations should be like, what kind of food to serve, how much drink you'll need, what kind of music to play and so on, if you know that it's an informal dinner for six good friends, as opposed to a big reunion for all your old college friends, or a glitzy party to celebrate your parents' 30th wedding anniversary. Also, if you're clear about what kind of an event you're holding and why, your guests will be, too. However adventurous we like to think we are, the truth is that we like to know more or less what to expect. That doesn't mean your guests don't want any pleasant surprises. They just don't want to turn up at a fancy dress party in black tie, that's all. Now is that *too* much to ask?

YOUR PERFECT EVENT

The type of event is crucial, but don't stop there. Ask yourself what kind of atmosphere you'd like to create. Is this a formal event? An informal one? Do you want people to make an effort with their outfits or is it an after-work come-as-you-are sort of thing? Visualise it. What does it look like? Sound like? Smell like? Taste like? You get the idea. Any gathering is a sensory event and, as host, you can determine what your guests will see, hear, feel, taste, smell.

Attention to detail is crucial, and it really is the key to making a so-so event special. Yes, even if you want something laid-back and informal. Having friends round for a pizza and video night? Try theming it – how about a scary movie evening? Rent out your movies beforehand, and cue up the really grisly parts. (The bonus if you have a DVD is that you can skip straight to your favourite scene.) Don't just think about the scary movies, have some scented candles burning, get spicy toppings for the pizzas and mix up some Bloody Marys to drink. Suddenly, a night in with friends becomes something a lot more memorable and fun.

Most people who hold events don't carefully think through what they want the end result to be. What happens? They end up hosting something that's often fine, but pretty forgettable. Entertaining can be hard work and, invariably, it will cost, too. If you're going to the effort of playing host, then you may as well do it well (and, ideally, get some return invitations while you're at it).

Traditionally, people have used social gatherings to celebrate certain fixed events: birthdays, national holidays like Christmas, weddings. As life becomes less formal and structured, and we're choosing to socialise more and more in our homes, we no longer seem to need a 'good reason'. If the weather's looking bright for the coming weekend, that's a good enough reason to have a barbecue. If most of your friends will be out of town over New Year, then a pre-New Year drinks party sounds great. People will have parties now to celebrate moving to a new home, leaving an old one, naming or christening ceremonies, and even the start of the new football season or a divorce being finalised (though those last two aren't necessarily linked!).

It's true that 'themed' parties or ones where a bit more thought has gone into the detail do tend to sound more interesting to guests, and so they're probably more likely to turn up. It's the difference between someone saying 'I'm just having a drinks party – would you like to come?' compared to 'I'm having a Hollywood cocktail party – are you free?' I know which I'd choose. For more on the pros and cons of themed parties, see Chapter 4.

DO I REALLY NEED A REASON TO PARTY?

Of course, you don't *have* to have a reason for getting friends together – even the fact that it's Friday will do. But if you want to really customise your event and make it that bit more special, just think of something you'd like to celebrate, then ask yourself *how* you'd like to mark the occasion. So, for example, you may want to have a house-warming party. That's straightforward enough. Or you could go one step further, and turn it into a decorating party for half a dozen friends. By way of thanks, you let them know they'll be plied with gourmet take-out from your local deli and champagne. Here are some other ideas:

→ An alfresco party to christen new garden furniture
→ A 1920s cocktail party
→ A kids' birthday party
→ A summer high tea
→ Friends for a coffee and cake morning
→ Birthday lunch for your mum
→ Romantic dinner for two
→ Dinner for the boss – if you really, really like them
→ Dinner for your team – if you're the boss, and they like you
→ Singles dinner party (every guest brings another single person)
→ Oscars party
→ Decorating party for new flat
→ Bring a dish party (result – you don't have to cook). These are very popular in the States, where they're known as 'pot luck dinners'. Let people know whether to bring sweet or savoury. You can even be specific and ask for 'something veggie/something with chicken' to make sure you end up with a good mix.
→ A girls'/boys' night in
→ Sunday pancake brunch for your brother/sister and their kids
→ An adoption party picnic to introduce a new family member

KNOW YOUR AUDIENCE

The first thing you need to think about when entertaining are the people that you want to invite. How many? Who? And why? (Is it a special occasion?) The kind of event you choose to have will depend to a certain extent on your guest list. If, for example, you want to hold a 10th birthday party for your niece and six of her friends, then that immediately helps you make some of your choices.

When thinking about your event, consider carefully who you'd like to invite and what they might feel comfortable with. What are the ages of the people you're inviting? What kind of things do they like doing? If you're going for fancy dress, are your guests likely to relish the thought or be put off coming? Is there anything they can't do or that would be inappropriate. Kids at a drinks party are as much of a mistake as are elderly relatives at a baseball picnic. The more themed or specific your event, the more important it is to know your audience and how they're likely to react. This is why most people go for characterless gatherings – apart from the effort it involves thinking through the detail, the truth is they're scared of getting it horribly wrong.

If you're unsure, of course, you can always sound people out to gauge their reactions. Have a quick word with your core group of guests, the people you'd really like there. Tell them the kind of event you want to hold. How does that sound to them? Would they come or would they find it off-putting? Do they think it would appeal to your other guests? Don't get bogged down – this isn't brain surgery. Most people know their friends well enough to be able to tell what kind of thing they'd find fun. After all, if they're friends of yours chances are you'll have similar tastes.

THINK THROUGH YOUR BUDGET

Money may make the world go round but most of us hate thinking about it. Especially when we'd much rather be having a good time. If you're planning an event, it's very easy to skip the money bit and not even consider how much the whole thing is going to cost you till you're at the supermarket checkout and feel a cold sweat coming on. But, yes you've guessed it: this bit is vital. Unless your surname is Getty, chances are you *need* to think about the budget for your entertaining.

This doesn't only apply if you're planning a big event like a wedding reception or a large birthday party. Even if you're having a few good friends round for pasta and salad, you must think through how much you can afford to spend. After all, there are so many choices these days – how will you be able to decide whether to splash out on home-made pasta or dried? Seriously, entertaining will always cost you, and the reason people don't do it more often is because they think it's going to cost them a lot, or they've had a bad experience with a dinner party that has cost them a small fortune. Entertaining really doesn't have to be expensive. But it's best to face up to facts early on in the planning process, otherwise you run the risk of your best-laid plans going pear-shaped. You don't want to spend a fortune on invitations, for example, and then find out that you don't have enough money left to make a decent meal. (See Chapter 6 for how to choose quality ingredients, at a reasonable price.) And you don't want to end up begrudging the fact that your guests want to open another bottle of wine.

For most of us, our budget will, to a certain extent, determine the kind of event we're able to have, where we have it and how many people we can realistically invite. There are all kinds of 'hidden' expenses when it comes to entertaining but that shouldn't put you off. They're only 'hidden' if you haven't thought them through. And you have, haven't you? Read Chapter 3 – by the end of it you'll be fully equipped to work out your budget (both your time and money) and have lots of cost-saving ideas. And we promise you won't look like a cheapskate.

CHOOSING YOUR VENUE

For most of us, much of our entertaining is done at home. There will, however, be occasions when your home isn't the best place to hold a gathering, and you need to think about hiring a venue or going elsewhere. This will depend on how many people you're inviting, how formal the event is, what the occasion is, and so on. Once you hire a venue, you are entering into a contract with someone and invariably will be employing staff to serve drinks/food and maybe even prepare the venue for you. Check out Chapter 11 for what to look out for when hiring professionals.

ALTERNATIVE VENUE IDEAS

Your garden: if you have a large enough space you can put up a mini-marquee or a gazebo. Or convince a friend or neighbour who has a big garden to have a joint party. If it's very sunny, these can provide great shade. Make sure you hire some portable, outdoor heaters for chilly nights. If you have a party outdoors, always have some kind of covering in case of rain.

A gallery/museum: check local ones rather than big, flash ones in town that tend to cost a fortune. Or try a small, local art gallery – perfect for a cocktail party.

A pub: many have function rooms upstairs, complete with bar and bar staff, that they hire out for a small fee. They will often also lay on food. Assuming you like the decor and the space is big enough, pubs often make great places for small birthday gatherings. Check out whether you can take along your favourite music and decorate it beforehand, to give it a personal touch. Some pub rooms are large so make sure you invite enough people to make it feel cosy. There's nothing worse than a half-empty venue.

Your favourite local restaurant: some restaurants will let you hire out the whole venue for the evening, while they lay on a set menu for you and your guests. This is a perfect solution if you want to provide dinner for a large group. Most people will be more than happy to pay, so don't feel you have to foot the whole bill. Put a certain amount of money behind the bar, or let everyone know that the first few rounds of drinks are on you (which of course means they pay for the rest). Only hire a restaurant as a venue if you know it well and have eaten there several times. If you're a regular customer, the staff will feel more committed to providing a good service, too.

Members' bar or club: if you or a friend have private membership to a bar or club, you'll probably be able to use their facilities for events. These will often be somewhere central and so make life easier for all concerned.

Manor house/stately home/historical building: now we're talking serious money, but if your budget can stretch to it, many historical buildings hire out rooms for parties and functions. You may not be able to customise the venue as you'd like (they probably won't let you hang balloons from their medieval wrought iron chandeliers) but if you're looking for something formal and impressive, these venues can't fail. (There tend to be many restrictions in venues like these so check our list below for questions to ask.)

If you're looking for a venue, ask yourself:

What kind of room do I need? Do I need more than one room? Should it be indoors or outdoors?

How much can I afford?

How many people can comfortably fit inside? Will they be seated or standing?

Is smoking allowed? Also, some venues don't allow drinking red wine, so check this.

What kind of alcohol licence do they hold? What time must we finish the event?

Am I allowed to put up decorations? When will I have access to the room to do this?

Will I be expected to take them down at the end of the evening or can I come back the next day?

Will I be expected to clean up straight after the event? Can I pay someone else to do this?

Is music allowed? Any restrictions on what kind?

If I'm hiring a DJ, will there be space/ample electricity supply for his/her equipment?

How will my guests get to and from the venue? How will we arrange cabs at the end of the evening?

Check the toilet facilities – are there enough for the numbers you're entertaining?

Meet the person in charge, usually the venue or banqueting manager. Make sure they understand what you want and are confident that they can provide it. Do they have experience in holding this kind of event?

Visit your venue at the time your event will take place as well as during the day. If it's an evening event, see what it looks like by night.

YOUR FIVE-MINUTE CHECKLIST

→ Why am I having the event?
→ How many people do I want to invite?
→ How much money do I want to spend?
→ How much space do I have?
→ Do I need to hire a venue or am I having this at home?
→ Will I be providing food or just nibbles?
→ Will I be providing alcohol? Soft drinks?
→ What time of day is the event?
→ How long will it go on for?
→ How would I sum up the atmosphere I want to create in three words? (e.g. funky, cool, laid-back.)
→ How am I going to achieve that feel?
→ Do I need to plan entertainment?
→ What kind of music will I play?

MISTAKES TO AVOID

I AM A VERY POPULAR PERSON AND THIS PARTY WILL PROVE IT

A common mistake is to invite everybody you've ever met to your
gathering. Keep in mind that quality is better than quantity and if
you invite hordes of people you will exhaust yourself and end up
spending a small fortune, too. How many people attend your party
is *not* a sign of your popularity – it's a sign of how many people you
know. Don't tell me you've never been to a party held by someone
you don't really like. We're social animals. If someone invites us
somewhere, we tend to show. Think of the best party you've been to
– was it one where there were scores of people you didn't know, or
one where it felt like an exclusive set of guests?

MY CULINARY SKILLS SURPASS DELIA SMITH'S AND MARTHA STEWART'S

Don't prepare ridiculously complicated food, then forget to keep the
music playing, dim the lights and talk to your guests. People don't go
to dinner parties for the food. Yes, they want to eat, but they just want
something decent and tasty. They're turning up to see *you*, maybe
meet some new people and have a good time. Keep that in mind, and
see Chapter 6 for making fantastic food that is easy and quick.

THIS IS GOING TO BE THE BEST PARTY IN THE WORLD. EVER...

A recipe for disaster is the host who thinks theirs is the party to
end all parties. Why would you want to put yourself under that kind
of stress? If you are desperate to make this *the* event of the year/
decade/lifetime, you'll be so wound up before anyone arrives that
your guests will feel it as soon as they enter. As host, it's your job
to create a relaxing atmosphere in which people can enjoy
themselves. It's not your job to give them the ultimate life
experience they'll never forget, all in one evening. Chill. Of course
you want it to go well, and it will if you relax and enjoy yourself.
Your guests will follow your lead.

2 INVITATIONS – WHO TO INVITE AND HOW

Any good host will tell you that your guests are the most important part of entertaining. Knowing who to invite, however, and who not to, can be difficult.

Of course, if you're holding a big family occasion, such as a wedding anniversary party for your parents, then your guest list practically writes itself. There will be people who automatically get invited because they're a member of the club – they belong to your family.

But if you're throwing something a bit more open-ended, like a 30th birthday party for yourself, then you have to sit down with your address book and really think through who you want there. Doing this without getting tied up in knots can be tricky – in an ideal world we'd like to throw our doors open in a magnanimous fashion and invite everyone we know. But space, practicality and budget won't allow it.

I DON'T KNOW WHO TO INVITE

Ask yourself why you're holding the event and – if it's a special occasion – what it's celebrating. Who absolutely *has* to be there? Is there anyone without whom the event wouldn't work? If so, make sure those people are available on the dates you're planning your event before you start inviting anyone else.

The reason many of us get stressed about guest lists, is because we either want to invite more people than we can or we don't want to invite a certain person but are worried we'll cause offence. Here's a secret: you can do whatever you like. You're the host, you're calling the shots.

HOW TO INVITE GUESTS

1. MAKE A LIST

Even if your event is an informal dinner with a few friends, make a list of who you want there. Don't invite anyone yet. Just look at the list and think about how well these people know each other, if at all. Do you think they'll get on? Do they have any common interests? Perhaps they always get invited to the same events? Would it be more interesting to invite someone new that nobody else knows? If you do this, it's best to invite a couple of people that are new to the group rather than one new person who may end up feeling a bit of an 'outsider'.

Most of us socialise with the same people most of the time, and invite the same people into our homes time and again. That can be just as successful as, with good friends, the anticipation of knowing you're going to have a good time is half the fun. But there's nothing to stop you inviting someone you don't know very well and it can make for a more interesting evening. If you've met someone at a party through a friend, say, invite the friend and ask them to invite the other person on your behalf. Life would be dull if we always stuck to the same crowd.

The less formal the event, the less it matters that you have a boy/girl mix. But be sensitive to your guests. Don't invite an unhappily single guy to a dinner with two besotted couples. And don't assume that all couples want to mix exclusively with other couples. They really don't.

2. LOOK AT NUMBERS

Remember, this is not a popularity contest. It isn't about how many people you can squeeze into your venue. Think about the kind of event you're holding and how many people would be appropriate. And ask yourself how many people you can manage. If you're cooking lunch or dinner, are you really geared up for more than six? Do you have enough table space? Chairs? Cutlery? Crockery? Glasses? (And we haven't even started on the food and drink, of course.) Catering for a crowd doesn't have to be expensive but the more people you invite the more complicated the event becomes, the more organising it takes and the more exhausting it is. So keep this in mind (and see Chapter 3, which will help you decide what you can afford).

Also think about how much time you want to spend planning this event.

It's easy to get carried away and let what was an intimate dinner for four friends become dinner for twelve. That's not a problem as long as you have the time, money and energy to deal with that, and as long as you accept that the quality of the food and drink will probably have to decline a bit in proportion to the rise in numbers. So instead of smoked salmon for four, you may be looking at pasta for twelve. This isn't necessarily wrong – it just changes the tone of the event.

3. THINK CAREFULLY ABOUT THE TYPE OF EVENT

You may already know you want friends round for dinner. Look at your numbers – are there too many people? Either scale down the numbers or change the event into something less formal (say a buffet where people can help themselves and you don't have to worry about seating everyone round one table).

Unless you're pretty confident in the kitchen, and always get your timing spot-on, I'd avoid cooking a formal sit-down meal for more than about six people. If you're inviting more than that, it's easier to be less formal about it. Make several big dishes everyone can help themselves from, letting guests sit anywhere they want: in the garden, in the living room, wherever there's space. Entertaining like this also takes the pressure off getting everything ready at the same time, as some dishes can arrive at the table later than others and it doesn't matter. (See Chapter 15 for ideas on catering for a crowd.)

4. LOOK AT YOUR LIST AGAIN

Take a final look at your guest list and amend if necessary before you start inviting. Have a few people on a 'reserve' list in case someone can't make it (obviously you don't tell them they're on the subs bench!). If someone drops out on the day, it isn't the end of the world. Just remember never to invite them again, unless they have a very good excuse! Never invite anyone at the last minute to make up numbers unless they are a *very* good friend and you can be honest about the fact that they're replacing someone who's not showing up.

THE INVITATIONS

Whether you send out formal, written invitations or invite people by phone, there are some obvious basics that need to be communicated.

1. THE KIND OF EVENT YOU'RE HOLDING

Will there be food provided or just nibbles? People want to know whether to eat beforehand. Is it to celebrate a specific occasion or just for the hell of it?

2. WHERE IT IS

Supply a map or directions if necessary. If you've hired a venue, make sure it is central enough for everyone (see Chapter 1 for tips on hiring a venue). If there's anyone in your group who's disabled, will there be access? If you're inviting guests from out of town, offer to put them up for the evening if you can, or supply the names of some good bed and breakfast hotels nearby (check out the B&Bs beforehand to make sure they're up to scratch). If you have lots of people using the same B&B, you may be able to negotiate a discount for them.

3. WHEN

Day, date, time. The more formal the occasion, the more notice you need to give people as, presumably, it matters more if they can come. For a wedding, you should let people know a couple of months beforehand, at least. For a dinner party, two or three weeks is ideal. If you are not able to send out your invitations immediately, ask people to 'save the date' – make sure they don't make plans for that date. Then get back to them as soon as you can to confirm if the event is being held on that date and that they are now officially invited. If you're holding a big house party and want to make sure enough people will be around, come up with a couple of possible dates then ring your guests to see which they can do. Get them to 'save the date' then get back to them to confirm.

4. WHAT TIME

It's an unwritten rule that most people seem to understand, that the more formal the event the more important it is that they're on time. Nobody wants to turn up late for a wedding to have missed the bride and groom exchanging vows, but if you're at a drinks party for fifty, arriving half an hour after stated on the invitation isn't a disaster. In fact, some hosts deliberately ask people to come at different times to big events, so that the flow of guests can be staggered and the venue doesn't get too crowded. Be specific about time when inviting people. If it's a dinner party, say it's 7.30 for drinks and dinner is at 8.30. That gives people a one-hour window in which to turn up.

For a large party or a daytime event, it's perfectly OK to say what time the event will be winding down. You don't have to say 'and we'd like you to leave by 7 p.m. please'! Just say, 'we'd love you to join us for a picnic – it will probably run from around 3–7 p.m.'. Far from finding it rude, guests really don't mind. In fact, most people like to know what the parameters are so they can plan their time accordingly.

Nobody wants to be the first to arrive at a party, but someone has to be. If you're worried that it won't get started till much too late (because everyone is waiting till they think it will be crowded before they arrive) then state on your invitation that you'll be giving a prize for the first arrival.

5. WHAT TO WEAR

Most of the time you probably won't need to think about this, but if you want your guests to make a special effort, or if there's a dress code at the venue you're hiring, you must let people know. There's nothing worse than turning up for an event and feeling really out of place. You don't always have to spell it out – if you say you're having 'an elegant drinks party – dress accordingly' people can interpret that as they want. Really what you're saying is 'make an effort', and everyone understands that.

Remember that dress codes can put people off attending, so knowing your audience, again, is vital here. Some people loathe fancy dress, others hate not being able to wear jeans if it's the weekend. Look at your guest list – who might be put off coming by your dress code? Does it matter?

6. WHAT TO BRING

Not many people would turn up at a party of any kind without having brought something, whether it's a bunch of flowers or a bottle of wine. That said, you can't expect everyone to do this. Some people are naturally generous, others just don't think that way, so there's no point being offended. After all, you've invited them to *your* house so why should *they* be supplying the drink? This is meant to be on you!

If you'd like guests to bring something, ask. Either write 'bring a bottle please' on your invitations, or just say, 'Would you mind bringing some wine?'

If someone turns up with a bunch of flowers, don't just put them down somewhere and forget them. However busy you are, make a point of putting them in a vase and placing it somewhere visible, but where it won't get knocked over. If someone brings chocolates, hand them round at the end of the evening.

7. HOW TO RSVP AND BY WHEN

I once went to party where only three guests turned up. Why? Because the host had invited everyone verbally, very casually and had said something along the lines of 'you don't need to let me know if you're coming – just turn up'. The result was a table full of uneaten food, an empty flat and an excruciating few hours for me and the other two guests. Rule number one when inviting guests: if you make people feel you're not bothered if they come they probably won't. Rule number two: always get them to RSVP.

If people can't give you a definite 'yes' or 'no' immediately, tell them when you'd like to know by. If they don't get back to you, call them and find out if they're coming. It's vital for planning food and drink that you know how many people to expect, and the bigger the event the sooner you need that information!

CAN I INVITE VIA EMAIL OR PHONE?

Yes. If your event is informal, there's no reason you can't. That said, receiving an invitation through the post is a lot more exciting. There's no reason why you can't phone or email a few guests first, making sure they save the date, and then tell them an invitation will follow in the post. This makes sure that the people you really want to be there will be there, and it also lets you build up the anticipation with a proper, formal invitation, too. Best of both worlds.

WHAT KIND OF INVITATION?

If you're sending a written invitation, it's a great chance to get your guests excited about the event. It's probably the first time your guests will know that you're planning something and, depending on what you choose to do, you can start creating your theme/atmosphere for the event right now. You can get ready-made invitations at high street stationers, you can get special ones printed up for formal occasions, like weddings, or you can even make your own.

Maria Hipwell and Liz Ellerton are founders of Lilies and Chips, who make bespoke invitations, cards and party paraphernalia. They say, 'Your invitation should get people excited and looking in their diaries. This is difficult to do verbally. A good invitation can get across your attitude and tone, and can set the scene so your guests know what kind of a party it will be. An email can be easily deleted, whereas an invitation sits around the house, building up a sense of anticipation. We put a lot of creativity into our invitations – each one is different because each party is different.'

Here's an example of how inventive you can get with invitations. For an architect's party, Lilies and Chips sent everyone a piece of the building block game, Jenga, with their name on it. All the guests were asked to come along and bring their personal piece of Jenga with them. At the party they built a huge tower block and tried to get into the *Guinness Book of World Records*. They're still waiting to hear whether they broke a record, but the point is that it was relevant (the architects involved are famous for building tower blocks) and fun.

Having invitations made up for you can be costly, though companies like Lilies and Chips will work with the budget you have (see Resources chapter for contact). If you're planning something very special, it's worth it. And if you have a theme for your event, the invitations can help follow that through.

Nobody knows that better than Victoria and David Beckham, though of course we're not suggesting you go to these extremes: to celebrate the World Cup, they held a charity event at their home with an oriental theme, as the games were being held in Korea and Japan. The invitations were tied with specially imported Japanese grass and cost £10,000.

SHALL I MAKE MY INVITATIONS?

Making your own invitations can save you money, but it helps if you're an artistic type who likes doing this kind of thing. If you are that way inclined, you can have a field day making your invitations. For a Christmas drinks party, cut out motifs from some wrapping paper, or send little wrapped-up matchboxes with the invitation folded up inside; if it's a Hallowe'en party, try some black card and glitter pens; for a beach picnic, send out seaside postcards as invitations, and so on.

A word of advice: don't underestimate the amount of time and effort it can take to make your own invitations. If you're delayed, you may end up sending them out too late. And you don't want to get so fed up of making them that, by the time you're halfway through, they've started to look like the doodlings of a toddler. Keep them simple and stylish. Or, if you're short on time, buy them.

MIXING GROUPS

Probably the most problematic part of making a guest list is knowing whether to keep groups of friends/family/colleagues separate or to mix them. Sorry, but there are no hard and fast rules. You really have to go on your guests' personalities and what kind of event it is. For a late-night dinner that might get a bit raucous, inviting some family members (like your parents, for instance) will immediately change the tone, so it's up to you whether you want that to happen. A family, daytime gathering tends to bore teenagers unless they have other teens of their age there, too. Toddlers and children are happiest at daytime events. And, unless you can swear not to talk shop all night, colleagues are probably best left to mix amongst colleagues.

The bigger the event, the less it matters if you mix groups, as chances are people will find other guests who are similar to themselves and get on fine. 'Concentrate on introducing people and take time doing it,' says Lizz Clarke, a Dale Carnegie trainer who's spent years helping employees learn how to network. She says, 'You have to make others feel comfortable. The worst party I ever went to was a housewarming where I wasn't introduced to anyone, there was only alcohol and I had to drive home. I never even saw the host!'

One of the things many of us worry about is the conversation drying up, especially if we invite people we don't know as well. 'Try not to be afraid of silences,' says Lizz. 'Don't panic – let it go companionably for a while. Just think positively and think of a positive thing to say. Introduce a chatty person to a quiet person – they are often best suited as the quiet person is under little pressure to talk. Follow the law of "opposites attract".'

YOUR FIVE-MINUTE CHECKLIST

→ Have I invited who I want rather than who I think I should invite?
→ Can I manage the numbers and the type of event I'm planning?
→ Will my guests like this kind of event?
→ Have I given guests all the information they need about the event (either verbally or on the invitation)?
→ Do they know how and by when to RSVP?

MISTAKES TO AVOID

I HAVE TO MAKE EVERYONE TALK TO EVERYONE

No you don't. You have to welcome people on arrival, tell them you're thrilled to see them and introduce them to any other guests around. When people attend functions they understand that a certain amount of effort will be expected of them – to mingle, to talk, to have a good time. You can't make people enjoy themselves. That's up to them.

I MUSTN'T KEEP INVITING THE SAME PEOPLE

It's good to mix friends and groups, but there's also a lot to be said for having a couple of friends who can be relied on to get the proceedings off to a good start. Some people are blessed with fantastic social skills and the ability to make others feel completely at ease. They don't have to be great raconteurs or comedians (though it often helps). These are the friends who are like gold dust. You know they will help any shy guests feel part of the group, and that they will help keep the whole proceedings going when you're in the kitchen checking on the food. Treat these friends well.

I SUPPOSE I HAVE TO INVITE X...

No, you really don't. It's never going to be the event you want it to be if the wrong people are there. Don't invite anyone you don't want there. What's the worse that can happen? They'll hear you had a party and they didn't get invited. They'll get annoyed. They may even confront you about it. Chances are they won't. You may never hear from them again. You won't have to worry about it next time, will you?

Word of advice: you *cannot* invite one part of a couple to something and not the other, unless it's a girls'/boys' night in, in which case you can get away with it. Ditto people's children: the only time you can ask someone to an event but ask them not to bring their children is if it's an obviously 'grown-up' gathering, like a cocktail party or a Saturday evening dinner. Make it clear if the children aren't invited. Ask about babysitters, which is a subtle way of getting the message across without causing offence.

3 BUDGETING YOUR MONEY AND YOUR TIME

Don't skip this chapter! Money is something most of us don't like to think about in everyday life, let alone when it comes to planning a party. It's boring and we'd much rather start thinking about what drink we need to buy, or planning our outfit. But whether you're planning a big bash or a casual evening with friends, you absolutely *have to* think about money before you start spending. Why? Otherwise you'll end up spending more than you planned to (had you planned it at all, of course) or you'll spend more than you actually have.

We're not suggesting you turn into Scrooge – the whole point of entertaining others is that it's a generous-spirited thing to do – but entertaining can be horribly expensive if you don't set yourself some limits and stick to them. If you skip the budgeting side of things, it isn't that difficult for a small gathering to turn into a very expensive affair. That's why many people don't bother entertaining – they assume it's going to be expensive. Of course it doesn't have to be, and this book will arm you with lots of tips for saving money and time. But the reason many people do overspend when entertaining is simply because they haven't got a budget in the first place, and without the limits that a budget imposes they just keep spending. Then when they add up what the whole event has cost them, they realise that it would have been cheaper to take that small group of friends out to a top restaurant.

HOW MUCH DO I WANT TO SPEND?

This is the first question to ask yourself when planning your event. Note, that the question isn't 'how much can I afford?'. Just because you can, in theory, afford to spend a certain amount doesn't mean you necessarily choose to do so. As a general rule of thumb, the more formal the event the more it will cost (as you'll probably want to serve higher quality food and wine). Any event that involves hiring a venue will, of course, cost you more than an event held at home, as will anything that requires hiring the professional services of others.

THE FOLLOWING QUESTIONS WILL HELP YOU DECIDE HOW MUCH TO SPEND

1. DO YOU ENTERTAIN A LOT?

'Entertain' means anything from friends coming round for pizza, to a full-blown, dress-up dinner party. If you are always inviting people to events at your house, try to estimate how much this costs you on average each time. Can you afford that? Do you *want* to be spending that? We're not going to tell you how to run your life, but it's pretty obvious that if an overdraft is a normal state of affairs for you, then an event that's less formal may be better. Then you can ask friends to bring along a contribution.

2. WHAT KIND OF EVENT ARE YOU HOLDING?

Keep it simple if money is tight. It doesn't have to mean you scrimp; if you're holding a dinner party, just cook one great course and buy a lovely dessert. (See Chapter 6 for ideas on food and how to impress without spending a fortune.) Make sure that the event you want to hold corresponds with what you can afford.

3. HOW MANY PEOPLE ARE YOU INVITING?

Again, do a reality check on what you can afford, and look at Chapter 2 for tips on writing your guest list. One of the main reasons we end up spending more than we want to on entertaining is because we just can't stop inviting people! Accept that you can't have everyone at this event. Have a separate event in six months and invite the rest.

4. HOW 'SPECIAL' IS THE OCCASION?

Is it being held because of a 'life event', such as a significant birthday, wedding, anniversary or christening? If it is, it can be difficult to cut costs as your guests (often family) will have certain expectations. It may also be one of the few times they ever all get together, and as such everyone will want it to be an all-singing, all-dancing event. Try to get someone to hold the party with you and share expenses. Failing that, discuss having a less formal affair. I went to a summer naming ceremony that was a barbecue held in someone's garden. Much nicer than a stuffy reception in some anonymous hotel, a lot less formal and a great deal less expensive, too.

5. CAN YOU SPLIT THE COSTS WITH A FRIEND?

Throwing a joint party can be a good way of saving money. A few things to keep in mind, though: agree upfront what kind of party, numbers you can both invite, what each will contribute (both in time and money) and who is in charge of what. Agree on basics like the kind of food, drink, music, atmosphere and decor you want. Both be there to set up at the start and clear up at the end or the next day.

6. CAN YOUR GUESTS CONTRIBUTE IN ANY WAY?

Most people will ask, so do take advantage of this or ask them. Depending on how formal your event is (and how well you know your guests) you may want to ask them to bring along one dish. This works particularly well if you're having a big buffet or a barbecue. If you're holding a dinner party, you can ask them to bring along a course, such as a dessert, or some lovely ciabatta bread. This is only a good idea if you know them well and know they won't mind. Some cultures – Greek, Italian, Spanish – won't think twice about bringing food along, whereas others may feel that you should provide it all. Your guests can contribute in different ways, of course, such as bringing alcohol and even making compilation tapes or CDs of music for a party.

WHAT DO I NEED TO PAY FOR?

Here's a list of items that may cost you, depending on the formality of your event. Write the cost next to each item and then make yourself a running total so you can see how much the event is costing you so far. If it's turning out too expensive, you still have time to change your plans and cut back. This isn't a definitive list – you may need to add to it depending on your event.

Invitations

Postage

Decorations

Flowers

Food

Drink

If you're calling in the professionals:

Caterer

Serving/waiting staff

Photographer

DJ/music

Venue costs

Hire of crockery, glasses, etc.

SOME COST-SAVING IDEAS

→ Use seasonal food that's locally produced only. Anything out of season that has been flown from the other side of the world will cost you more.

→ Buy drink from warehouses/wine merchants who operate a drink or return policy. They will often give you a discount if you buy in bulk. Worth doing if you entertain a lot.

→ Hire glasses from your local off licence, rather than buy them. Most places will let you have them for free if you're buying your drink from there. The deal is you return them the next day and pay for what you break.

→ Don't buy special decorations for a party – bring out your Christmas fairy lights. If you or a friend has a garden, raid it for inspiration (ivy draped around a fireplace looks good all year round).

→ Candles, especially tea lights, are an inexpensive way of creating a great atmosphere.

→ Borrow before you hire or buy. If you need blankets for picnics, skewers for barbecues, an ice bucket for a cocktail party, ask around and one of your friends is bound to have the equipment you need, and will be happy to lend it. To save any stress, collect it a few days before the event.

HOME-MADE HORRORS

When trying to save money, the temptation is to go into 'home-made overdrive' and do everything ourselves. There's nothing wrong with that – if you happen to be an incredibly versatile, gifted individual. But most of us aren't. Most of us are good at a couple of things, and should know to leave the others well alone. So before you decide to make your own invitations or bake that three-tier chocolate cake you like the look of, stop and think:

Have you ever done this before?

Have you been successful?

If you haven't, can you do a practice run several days before the event?

What happens if your home-made creation goes wrong?

Do you still have time to buy an alternative?

Will the alternative end up costing you more?

TIME – YOUR BIGGEST ENEMY

Time is one of those things you just don't notice until it's gone. And once it's gone, only money will bring it back. Let me explain. Imagine it's Christmas Eve and you haven't done any of your shopping. It's almost 5 p.m. and you've got an hour left before the shops close. What do you do? You panic buy, of course. You buy up anything and everything and end up spending a huge amount more than you ever intended.

The same applies to entertaining. If you don't plan ahead, you panic buy, spending more than you can afford. The bigger the event the more important it is to plan ahead, as you'll have more to organise. For example, if you're planning a wedding reception and you've set aside £300 for the cake, leaving it too late to find a cake maker means you'll end up spending more. If anyone provides a service for you faster than they normally would, they will charge you way over the usual price. Basically, they've got you over a barrel and you have little, if any, bargaining power. Every event benefits from planning ahead. It gives you a chance to find the best value everything – from invitations, food and drink, to flowers and music.

YOUR TIME – THE OTHER COST

When thinking about costs, don't just think about how much money you want to spend on this event, consider how much of your time you are willing to devote to it, too. How busy are you? What are you happy to do for yourself, and what would you rather buy ready-made, or pay someone else to do? The bigger, more formal the event, the more important it is to consider calling in the professionals, like caterers or waiting staff. After all, you don't want to be handing round trays of drinks at your own wedding reception! It's a false economy to think you can get away without professionals at big events. For tips on how to hire them and what to look out for, check out Chapter 11.

HOW MUCH TIME CAN IT POSSIBLY TAKE?

Even when entertaining on a small scale, don't fall into the trap of underestimating how much time certain things will take. It's a fact of life, that the things we're good at are easy and seem to take no time at all, while the things we're not so good at will take hours. So if you are a great cook and enjoy cooking, by all means go ahead and make three courses. But only if you will love doing it, know you'll get good results and won't end up frazzled. There's nothing worse than a grumpy, tired host.

If you don't want to spend ages in the kitchen, take advantage of the number of timesaving recipes and ingredients around. Prepare beforehand, whether it's setting out your glasses for a drinks party or decorating a room the night before. Even the busiest, most undomesticated person can entertain these days, as there's a huge range of deli foods available, caterers and, if it's a less formal event, takeaways.

YOUR FIVE-MINUTE CHECKLIST

→ Decide how much you want to spend.
→ Check this against the kind of event you're planning and numbers you intend to invite – is it realistic?
→ Planning ahead will save you money – start as soon as you can.
→ Enlist the help and contributions of others.
→ How much of your time do you want to spend on this event?
→ For larger, more formal events, consider calling in the professionals.

MISTAKES TO AVOID

I'M GOING TO HAVE WHAT I WANT AND TO HELL WITH THE COST

Unless you're Elton John, don't go down this road. Your money will run out. You will end up having the most exquisite, handmade invitations and serving cheese and pineapple to your guests. There's nothing wrong with humble fare, but don't dress up your event to be something it's not. You'll annoy your guests and nobody will know what's going on.

I DON'T HAVE TIME TO PLAN – THE BEST EVENTS ARE ALWAYS SPONTANEOUS

Spontaneity can be great and it *can* work. But planning will make your event that much better. It's the difference between pulling something together at the last minute with whoever happens to be around, and creating something that sparkles and will be remembered for all the right reasons.

I'M GOING TO CUT CORNERS EVERYWHERE – WHAT DO THEY EXPECT?

Don't bother. Really. The whole point of holding an event is to get people together and make them feel good about life. Having their wine rationed to one and a half glasses each won't do that. If you really can't afford to entertain, wait until you can. Or share costs with a friend.

4 TO THEME OR NOT TO THEME?

A theme can be anything that characterises your party and gives it personality. It can be a colour – you may decide to decorate everything in black and white. It can be a venue – say you hire a boat for a party. Or even a dress code – tell your guests it's a 70s bad taste party. The more parties and events we attend, the more pressure there is for a host to make theirs different and memorable. If executed well, a theme can really help make your event stand head and shoulders above any others that year.

Theming a party takes a bit more effort, and shows thought. Your guests know that and that's why themed parties often feel 'different', because they've been carefully planned and the host has managed to create a sense of excitement around the theme. Also, themes help narrow down your choices as a host. They may help you decide on decor, lighting, food, drink and music, actually making the event easier to host in the long run.

'Themes work well because they give you something to hang the whole party on,' say Maria Hipwell and Liz Ellerton, founders of Lilies and Chips, a company that creates party themes. 'They can help you make decisions about the invitations, decorations, and so on. There are so many things to think about when organising a party; having a theme helps make life easier.'

GOOD REASONS TO THEME YOUR EVENT:

→ Memorability
→ Gives an event a sense of fun and gets everyone in the party mood
→ Great icebreaker if you're inviting people who don't know each other
→ Can make the 'same old crowd' events seem more special
→ Great opportunity for closet extroverts to show off
→ You can create a more cohesive event that 'hangs together' better
→ Kids love themes

That said, don't go thinking that theming an event is the answer to all your prayers. Themes can be tricky and come with their own set of problems.

THE PITFALLS TO AVOID

→ Choosing a theme your guests hate. You have to know your audience and judge accordingly. The more specific you are with the theme, and the more distinctive your event, the more chance there is that your guests will either love or hate it.

→ Tackiness. Themes (especially colour themes) can look a bit forced if taken too far. Nobody wants to eat black food, even if it *is* a black and white party. Danielle Nay is MD of Dr Party, a company that specialises in fabulous themed parties for private and corporate clients. She says, 'Food is the one area you should be careful with. If you're having a colour theme, avoid food dye. And blue cocktails I have a problem with – hire blue glassware instead. At Dr Party, we like to theme the food by focusing on how it's presented. It's not the food that's tricksy it's the presentation. We recently organised a party for the fashion designer, Karen Millen, with a Moulin Rouge theme. We made Parisian food in miniature, such as *coq au vin* and *duck à l'orange*, and put it on bowls in velvet usherette trays.'

→ Themes can feel like forced 'fun' if you misjudge your audience. You may prefer to create a more laid-back, elegant atmosphere.

→ Letting the theme take over the event. You'll get distracted and forget basic rules, like making sure that everyone feels at ease and has a drink.

→ Themes, like fancy dress, can be expensive for guests. If this is an issue, choose something simple like a black and white theme – everyone can find something in their wardrobe that's black or white. Danielle says, 'A dress code or colour code is by far the easiest and cheapest way to theme a party.'

→ Grown-ups sometimes get embarrassed. Your theme may stop people attending. If you're throwing a fancy dress party, certain guests may attend and decide not to take part. If that matters to you, make it clear on the invite (in the nicest possible way) that fancy dress is a must. If someone *does* turn up without having made the effort, you'll just have to grin and bear it. Don't send them home, however annoyed you are! Chances are they'll end up feeling out of place and leave early anyway.

HOW TO CHOOSE A THEME

The best way to think of a theme is to consider the event and the guest list and take it from there. Some events lend themselves to certain themes – a silver wedding anniversary, for example, could easily have a colour theme for the decorations and table settings. A kids' party is easy to theme as there are so many popular children's characters, as well as lots of party merchandise around that fits the bill. Just find out who the child's favourite character is. Manufacturers know this is a huge market, and chances are if you want paper plates for a Harry Potter party or hats for Bob the Builder, you won't have many problems finding them. (See the list of resources at the end of this book for details of where to go.)

If there's no obvious theme, let the occasion set the tone. Think about what kind of atmosphere you want to create. If you're going for a cool, funky feel, choose an appropriate theme. Maria Hipwell and Liz Ellerton, at Lilies and Chips, say, 'Themes can be very simple. At one party we got some of those fridge magnets with words on them and invited everyone to write a sentence. It eventually made up a story – not the cleanest story, it has to be said! But it was very funny. After the party we typed it out and sent it to all the guests as a reminder of the party.'

Choosing a theme that ties in with a culture or country is fairly easy to pull off. Interiors stylist, Carl Braganza says, 'You might want to have an Indian theme, for example, if you're having an Indian meal. There's so much you can do. Think about all the bright, clashing colours associated with India and take your inspiration from there. Scatter rose petals, coloured sequins or bindis over the table. Tie the napkins with pink ribbon or gaudy gold trim. Make a name place for everyone and stick a bindi on each one. Have fun with it.' (For more ideas on decor, see Chapter 5.)

And do be bold. To make a theme really work, says Danielle, you need to go overboard with the decor. 'If you're having a Moroccan theme at home, for example, it's no good just having two cushions – you need a dozen. It's about piling it on so the theme is obvious.

'Also, drink is a good way to extend a theme. If you've got a Hollywood theme or a cartoon character theme, get everyone to come dressed in character. You can give the drinks names that reflect your theme. Put the glasses on decorated trays. You can buy some great wrapping paper these days – just go to your local printing shop and get it laminated, then you can stick it to a tray.'

When thinking this all through of course it's crucial that you consider your guests and what they're likely to find appealing. Common interests are a great way to think of a theme. So, for example, if all your friends love football, why not have a pizza and beer get-together to celebrate the start of the new football season? Ask everyone to come dressed in their favourite team's football top. There you go – you've got a theme.

If you and your friends love romantic comedies, have a 'rom-com' sleepover, where everyone gets changed into their pyjamas and eats ice cream and marshmallows while watching Meg Ryan movies. Or have a 'heart-throbs' evening where everyone gets to show an excerpt from their favourite black and white movie. The possibilities are endless. (For more ideas on what kind of event to hold, see Chapter 1.)

Choose a theme that reflects your passions and interests. If you know about a subject you'll throw yourself into organising the event and it will end up a lot more fun. Don't forget that that's the point – fun. As soon as a themed event starts being a chore you know you've either chosen the wrong theme or taken it too far.

SO HOW FAR IS TOO FAR?

You can theme to your heart's content but remember this: a theme is supposed to give a party an extra twist. It's something to focus on, for all your guests to feel excited about before arriving and to act as some kind of ice breaker. It isn't meant to be a pain, a huge expense or get ridiculously out of hand.

'Bad themes,' says Danielle, 'are the ones that are too subtle. Sometimes, I'm invited to corporate events that are trying to communicate something really complex with themes that feel irrelevant. So they might have, for example, one roulette table or a stilt walker. Don't have anything arbitrary, especially if you're spending serious money on it.'

WARNING SIGNS THAT YOU'VE TAKEN YOUR THEME TOO FAR

→ You can't remember why you're holding the party.
→ You've spent more time trying to get the right decorations than you have spent thinking about the food, drink and guests.
→ The theme has become overly complicated, stressful and caused you major expense or worry.
→ The theme doesn't reflect you or your interests in any way, nor those of your guests.

→ There's no room for manoeuvre – everything has to fit around the theme. Unless you have unlimited money, a good, workable theme should be flexible. It should *help* you with your decisions, not hinder them.

SOME GREAT THEME IDEAS

Here are some themed events that tend to be popular with a 20–30 something crowd. How far you take them is up to you.

→ A Hallowe'en goth party: 'dress scary'.
→ A Eurovision party: everyone is allocated a different country and asked to bring along a relevant national dish, as well as dress in the colours of their national flag.
→ A deco cocktail party: martinis, elegant dresses, black tie.
→ School disco: everyone comes in an old uniform and you play 'classics' from your school days on the stereo.
→ A glamorous Oscars party: come as your favourite movie star, have some popcorn, nibbles and champagne and watch the Academy Awards.
→ Murder Mystery dinner party: you can buy Murder Mystery games, complete with clues and characters, from most game stores. Guests are sent details of their characters beforehand, turn up dressed as that person and act accordingly. The host serves various courses between the revelations. (Great idea if your guests are all extroverts.)
→ Tea party: if you're a dab hand at home-made cakes, having friends round for high tea is a fun way to entertain.
→ Holiday party: just back from Morocco? Prolong that holiday feeling. Invite friends for a Moroccan meal and show them your holiday snaps. Even better if they went with you.

If you're still stuck for inspiration, have a look at this American website **www.partyplansplus.com** which should give you plenty of ideas. Americans love theming parties and, although some of these ideas are over the top (and perhaps not quite cool enough for what you're planning), this website shows how easy it is to take a theme and run with it.

If you're short on time and inspiration, you could buy your theme ready-made. Many large stationers and party shops sell merchandise packs that are themed. The items can include anything from tablecloths, paper napkins, cups and plates, to themed games and even outfits. They'll have the character or 'event' printed on them (e.g. 'Happy 21st'), so they're a great way of making the event feel special. These party packs work particularly well, however, when it comes to children's parties (as children tend to like 'character' themes, like Barney the Dinosaur or Harry Potter). See the Resources chapter for stockists.

There's no shame in buying a ready-made theme pack, as long as you accept that it will often give your event a less exclusive feel. Steer away from these packs if you have any aspirations for hosting a very sophisticated one – you're better off just colour-theming a smart 25th wedding anniversary with silver and white, rather than hanging up balloons that yell 'Happy 25th Wedding Anniversary'. The truth is there really is no right or wrong when it comes to theming. It really comes down to your personal taste and what *you* like. See the British website, **www.partybox.co.uk** for some ideas on themes for adult parties, and **www.partyproductsdirect.co.uk** for a good range of themed products. For more ideas on children's parties, see Chapter 16.

And, should you ever win the Lottery, here's how you can theme your party in style. Victoria and David Beckham recently hosted a Japanese-themed charity garden party (to commemorate England's participation in the World Cup). Event organiser and party maestro to the stars, Andrew Chance, saw the theme through from beginning to end. There were 60,000 orchids specially flown in and a Japanese garden was created in the grounds of their house. The Beckhams even had a replica of an oriental bridge installed. The entertainment consisted of Japanese Kabuto drummers, and geisha girls greeted guests on arrival. The menu was, of course, oriental too, and the party has gone down in history as the Beckhams' 'Gucci and Sushi' party. Oh, we can dream.

YOUR FIVE-MINUTE CHECKLIST

→ Choose a theme that reflects you, your guests or the event you're celebrating.

→ Keep it simple and don't take it too seriously, or you'll end up getting stressed.

→ Make sure you consider how your guests will take to the theme. Will they like it? Can they afford it? Ask around before you start inviting, if you're at all unsure.

→ Let people know on the invitation that it's a themed party and what, if anything, they need to do.

> → Don't go mad with a theme. It'll end up costing you too much in time and money. And don't let it distract you from the main business in hand, which is, of course, having a good time.

MISTAKES TO AVOID

I MUST THINK OF A THEME, I MUST THINK OF A THEME . . .

If you can't think of a theme, don't have one. Themed parties are great if you're bursting with ideas and have friends who love taking part in that kind of thing, or if the idea comes easily because it's obvious. But there's no rule that says you *have* to have a theme. As long as your event reflects you and caters to your guests' needs, it will be fab.

I'M GOING TO SPEND SO MUCH TIME ON THE DETAIL – THIS PARTY WILL BE GREAT

You may think that searching for days for the exact shade of green for your paper napkins is a good use of your time but trust us, it isn't. The reason is that you probably don't have that time to spare. And something else will fall by the wayside, like buying the food or, God forbid, inviting the guests.

I'M GOING TO HAVE A THEME, BUT NOT TELL ANYONE

People like to know what kind of party they are going to. They don't want it sprung on them at the last minute. If your theme is a simple one – like red and gold decor for Christmas – then fine. You don't need to let everyone know. But if it's a Mexican dinner, or a formal, black tie event people need to know. They need to mentally prepare as well as actually prepare. And it's much more fun and adds to the anticipation of it all if you know you're going to a 'special' party.

I'LL HAVE A FEW THEMES AND SEE WHAT HAPPENS

Keep it simple, keep it clear. If you throw several themes together, your guests will be confused and you'll send out all kinds of strange signals. It will end up a mess, mark my words.

5 DECOR – THE LIGHTS, FLOWERS, TABLE AND PRETTY STUFF

This chapter is all about presentation. I don't know anyone who'd arrive at a dinner party in their pyjamas, yet so many people forget to 'dress' their home or venue when entertaining. And before you think you're not holding that sort of event (and therefore you can skip this section) *stop right there*! Every sort of event can benefit from dressing up. How far you take it is entirely up to you.

What's surprising is that 99 per cent of people who decide to entertain neglect decor, and yet there are some very simple ideas that will make your venue look fantastic. For minimum effort you really can get maximum results. And what's the point of putting all your energy into the food and drink, if your guests feel uncomfortable, or the room seems cold and unwelcoming? Your efforts will have been wasted. Decor helps set the tone, and it doesn't have to cost a fortune, either.

Because so few people bother with decor, anyone who does really stands out. A few well-placed vases of flowers or a beautifully decorated mantelpiece will always be commented on and admired. Of course, it always looks nice when you've made an effort, but the real reason decor works is because it shows you care. You've gone that extra mile to make your guests feel special.

WHAT IT IS AND WHY YOU NEED IT

Decor is anything that adorns or changes your surroundings. It can be the use of lighting, a handful of decorations, a vase of flowers, the way you set the table, even how you arrange the furniture. Interiors stylist, Carl Braganza works at *YOU* magazine, and spends much of his working week styling interiors for photo shoots. He says, 'Over time, you learn what the easiest things to do are that get the maximum effect. It's amazing how people react if you make an effort with the table and decor. It makes everything feel festive and much more like a party. Your guests start chatting, and it immediately breaks the ice.'

All of these have an initial visual impact and, as such, are important. Decor can be used to draw attention to certain aspects of a room or to disguise them. If you're holding your event at home, make the room/house feel different to the way it usually does. Many of your guests will have seen your home several times, so putting some thought into the decor can help you transform the familiar and create an entirely new feel. Decor can also help you carry through a party theme – whether it's a colour or a subject – and create a specific atmosphere.

How many times have you heard about the importance of making a good first impression – and the fact that people tend to judge you in the first nanosecond of meeting? Well the same applies to the event you're holding. As soon as people walk into your venue they get a 'first impression' – of you, the event and what kind of time they're going to have. Here's how to make it all as positive and special as possible.

LIGHTING

The Hollywood screen legend, Marlene Dietrich probably knew more about lighting photographs than some of Hollywood's leading photographers. She made it her business to understand what flattered and what didn't and would only allow photographers to light her in a specific way. What she understood was the power of lighting and the way it can soften edges or sharpen them. Applied to a venue, the right lighting can make a room feel warm, friendly and welcoming. Lighting can create the illusion of space or intimacy. Get the lighting wrong and you wreck the atmosphere. Remember those school discos with bright lights in the sports hall and a few sad balloons in the corner? There was no forgetting that you were in a sports hall because nobody had bothered to try to disguise the fact.

HERE'S WHAT LIGHTING CAN DO

Candlelight: traditionally for romantics, but candlelight is great for any event where you want to create a feeling of cosiness and intimacy. 'If you have a framed mirror,' says Carl, 'a good trick is to lie it flat on the table and place your candles on top. The reflection gives you double the glow.' Candles also work well for large, festive occasions, like weddings or Christmas. Place them in the middle of each table or around the perimeter of a room. If you're putting candles on a table, place them either to the side or below eye level (so your guests are still able to make eye contact. The same goes for flowers.) Make sure you keep an eye on candles throughout the night, especially if your event is being held in several rooms. Don't leave them unattended, and be particularly careful of curtains and any flower arrangements.

Flashing lights: if you're hiring a DJ, they may bring these along, or you can hire them. Flashing lights are usually different colours and add a feeling of pace, energy and excitement. They're the opposite of candlelight. You can hire them for your home, too, if you're holding a party where people will be dancing. Check the lights are for domestic use and aren't too powerful for your electricity supply first, or you'll blow a fuse. Make sure you have a demonstration in your home/venue or feel confident of how to use them before the day if you're the one responsible for them working!

Uplighters: lights that shine upwards can be used to create a feeling of space and are particularly good for small rooms. If you have a couple of anglepoise lamps, change the light bulbs to a low wattage and simply angle them upwards. You can buy clip-on lamps quite cheaply. If you want a room to look a bit cosier and smaller, point them into the room, at opposite corners (though be careful they won't end up glaring in guests' faces). Coloured bulbs can look good in uplighters and are a good idea if you're colour-theming your event.

Overhead light: avoid using your ordinary overhead light if possible, as it will be too bright for most events apart from daytime ones. If this really is all you can manage, consider changing the light bulb to a soft, coloured one or fit a dimmer.

Light dimmers: if you're holding your event at home, fit some dimmers. They're easy to install (switch off all electricity first!) and, when turned down, create a soft glow. They're also incredibly handy when you want guests to leave as you can gradually turn them higher and people will get the message. If they really won't go, there's nothing like a bright light to signal that the party is well and truly over.

Fairy lights: I'm a big fan of using fairy lights for almost any occasion. The plain white ones look the most stylish, though coloured lights can also look great, too, especially for kids' parties. People associate fairy lights with Christmas and festivities, so bringing them out for a dinner party or a wedding reception can feel really special. It doesn't even have to be a formal event. They can work well draped over a large potted plant, like a yucca or a cactus, across a mantelpiece or over a picture frame. Interweave some ivy through them, and a few tall candles – the possibilities are endless. Fairy lights can be used over and over again, so it's worth paying for good quality ones that you'll be able to get good use out of. I love them because they are a very simple way of creating a real sense of occasion. A friend of mine has them draped permanently over her bed. Enough said.

Large venues may offer you 'pea lights' which are tiny white lights, similar to fairy lights, often strung across a room. They're a great way to create a cosy feeling in an anonymous venue. At my wedding reception I had a 'pea light canopy' – several strings of tiny white lights coming from the outer edges of the room and converging in the centre. It worked well because the room had very high ceilings and the canopy was almost like having a fake roof above us, keeping the party contained and intimate. Years on, people never comment on how fantastic I looked, but they remember the pea lights.

If you want a similar effect at home, you can buy an illuminated 'net' from most electrical stores. They comprise of several tiny lights embedded in a mesh. Hang them across a window like a curtain for a starry effect.

Garden lights: weather permitting, an evening spent outdoors can be magical. Garden flares are just like large candles with spears in the end that you push into the soil. They're perfect for lighting any outdoor space, but be sure to keep them away from hedges, tall borders and any trailing plants. Or use garden candles that are in terracotta pots, dotted around or grouped in clusters. Get the ones that contain citronella to keep the mosquitoes away, and your guests will love you even more. Strings of coloured bulbs or fairy lights are also ideal for outdoor use, especially when there's a large area to cover. You must buy lights that are specifically wired for outdoor use though.

Whatever kind of lighting you choose, don't forget that you can change the effect throughout the evening. If your guests are invited for dinner, say, try some fairy lights and a dimmed overhead light while you have drinks, turn the light up slightly during dinner (so everyone can see what they're eating!) and then dim the lights further or use candles when you're onto the coffee. When it's time for them to leave, again you can turn the lights up gently.

FLOWERS

Gone are the days when flowers were just associated with romantic events like Valentine's Day and weddings. Today, they can be used for practically any kind of occasion. When you're entertaining, think about flowers and whether they'd work at your event. Show me someone who doesn't like flowers and I'll show you a misery guts. They tend to bring a smile to most faces, as we associate them with love and joy. Whether you're entertaining at home or at a venue, consider using freshly cut flowers as part of your decor. They could be anything from huge sunflowers set in large vases for a wedding reception or a delicate, hand tied posy at an intimate dinner.

Emma Morris is visual and creative manager at the prestigious Kenneth Turner, one of the most innovative and influential floral decorators around. She says, 'Flowers can help create an ambience for the whole evening, and paired with candle light they can have a very beautiful and dramatic effect. We like to put candles in the flower arrangements themselves so the candlelight flickers over the flowers and gives a mysterious quality.'

WON'T FLOWERS COST ME A FORTUNE?

Not necessarily. As they're usually associated with celebrations and gift-giving, we tend to think that flowers are an extravagance. They can be, but it all depends on what you're looking for and where you buy them. Try not to buy ready-made bouquets from newsagents or petrol stations. They often look stale and sad, and they've probably been sitting there for days.

Some supermarkets do sell fantastic bouquets but the prices are high. If time is short, and you're in there because you're doing the rest of your shopping for your dinner party/event, snap them up. But you'll get better value for your money by going to a local florist.

At a florist, you can choose exactly what you want and get them to make up a large bunch for you or even a small one as a table setting. Most good florists will get certain flowers in for you if you give them some notice.

There are some very stylish, expensive florists out there and if money is no object then do investigate them as they often offer a more unusual, interesting range of flowers than your local one will. If you're using a florist like this, make the most of their skills and ask for their advice on colours and flowers, and get them to arrange your bunch for you and hand-tie it. That way, you'll only need to pop it into a vase when you get home.

'Go for freshness and what's in season,' says Emma, 'and always buy from somewhere that's busy, as their turnover will be high and they'll be getting daily deliveries. If you're going to a florist, visit someone with a good reputation that you can trust. Then you know they're going to the market for you and picking the best quality. You're buying into their expertise.'

If money is tight, try going along to a flower market yourself. You'll have to be an early riser if you want to get the best ones, though at the end of the day you may snap up some bargains. In theory, buying flowers from a market can save you a lot of money if you're hosting a large event (like a wedding reception) but, what with problems of storage and arranging before the day, you'd have to be mad to do this. You've probably got enough to think about without this added pressure so it really is a false economy. Get a florist instead. If you're throwing a small party the same day or the next, however, visiting a market is a perfect way to fill your house with flowers without breaking the bank.

And, of course, if you have a garden think about bringing some of it indoors. Emma says, 'Don't be afraid to cut things from the garden – do what you feel is right for you.' Your arrangements don't have to just be floral of course. Ivy, honeysuckle or holly, can all work very well trailed over mantelpieces. If you're cutting flowers or greenery from the garden, do it on the day of your event as flowers in particular do seem to die more quickly than shop bought ones. It goes without saying that dead or wilting flowers are a definite no-no!

Emma says, 'Your flowers don't have be overly formal. A few very carefully chosen stems make all the difference. You can use containers that you have round the house like old medicine bottles, antique jugs, beautiful bowls you can float flowers or petals in.'

If you have some herbs in the garden, bring some sprigs of rosemary indoors, or cut some lavender and place it in a vase in the hallway. The smell will greet your guests on arrival and help mask any cooking smells. Carl says, 'Nobody has time to spend ages on decorating a place setting for a dinner party. Use something from the garden, such as a sprig of lavender tied to a napkin with twine. It's a sweet touch and is particularly good if you have guests who don't know each other, as it'll get them talking.'

Be careful with highly perfumed flowers like lilies, roses and freesias as they shouldn't be placed near anywhere you're serving food. The same goes for scented candles. Our sense of smell is closely linked to our taste buds and very fragrant flowers can make food taste odd.

WHICH FLOWERS TO CHOOSE

'Trends and colours evolve the whole time,' says Emma. You may want to follow a particular fashion, or just go for what you like. Flowers can help you carry through a colour theme or create a certain feel for your event. As with everything, think about what kind of event you're holding and what atmosphere you want to create. For example, a tea party for aunts and uncles is the perfect setting for a short, glass vase filled with roses or sweet William. Some brightly coloured gerberas would look great in a tall ceramic vase at a smart dinner party. And a few well-chosen, tall white lilies would work well in a chrome vase at a 20s cocktail party. Always go for flowers that are in season as they'll look better (they won't have flown miles to get to you) and will be cheaper, too.

If you haven't got a clue about flowers, it doesn't matter. There are no real rights and wrongs. Just choose something that fits in well with the rest of your decor. As a general rule, the more stylised the flower, the more contemporary the feel (gerberas, lilies, iris). Flowers that have rounder petals and a softer, more cottagey look, such as roses, peonies and hydrangeas will look more romantic and old-fashioned.

DO I HAVE TO 'ARRANGE' THEM?

If you're trying to create a modern feel to your event, you won't want something that looks too 'arranged'. In recent years, flowers have taken on a far less formal look. Perfectly proportioned, formal arrangements are fine for formal events, but if you're entertaining at home they will probably make your guests feel rather ill at ease.

Have fun with flowers and try various colours next to each other. A good trick is to choose just one or two colours and buy up various shades of these. And don't be scared of using strong colours that clash, like oranges, reds and mauves – as long as you limit it to two or three colours at the most. Personally, I'm not keen on mixing several colours and types of flowers as I think you end up with what's known as a 'mixed bouquet'; it has a bit of everything in it but is not really saying anything. So it ends up being just a bunch of flowers, rather than adding to the overall feel of your event.

A word of advice: women *love* flowers. If you're a man who's planning a romantic dinner for two, buy some fresh flowers for your house or the table. You'll score major brownie points.

SOME COLOURS THAT WORK WELL TOGETHER, AND THE EFFECT THEY GIVE:

Reds and pinks: warm, romantic

Oranges and mauves: vibrant, daring

Whites and yellows: fresh, springlike

Greens and yellows: fresh, springlike

Pinks, lilacs and blues: soft, feminine

And don't forget that foliage can look just as good in a vase as flowers can.

WHICH VASE?

Before buying your flowers, think about where you're going to place them. There's no point buying tall, elegant lilies if your only vase is a short, round bowl. And remember, you don't have to just use vases. You may have a lovely old water jug or a pretty glass that can be used.

TIPS

→ The taller the flowers the taller the vase that you need, as you have to provide enough support for the stems.

→ Always measure your flowers against your vase before cutting, to make sure you don't cut too far down.

→ Cut at an angle to allow flowers to drink in as much water as possible. Use a knife or pruner, as scissors damage the stem and stop it allowing enough water through.

→ Get rid of all leaves below the water line. This stops bacteria breeding and helps the flowers live longer.

→ Change water every few days and each time cut your stems back a bit too.

→ Avoid putting flowers in the sunlight or near heat.

→ If your flowers are top heavy and threatening to tip over your vase, add some pebbles or marbles to the bottom of the vase to weigh it down before filling with water.

→ Don't place vases of flowers around a children's party, unless you can keep them well out of reach (and there are no chairs around that can be climbed on!).

→ If you're having a formal event, with a welcome desk/reception area, always have some flowers on the table to greet people as they walk in.

WHICH VASES/CONTAINERS FOR WHICH FLOWERS?

Short and squat vase (a round glass bowl-type vase): suits roses, dahlias, sweet William, ranunculus and hydrangea. Cut the stem to the height of the vase and only let the bloom stick out of the top.

Urn vase (narrow neck and wide rim): suits heavy flowers like lilies, orchids and gerberas.

Tall and narrow: suits sunflowers, snapdragons and gladioli.

Bud vase: for one flower only, works well with roses and peonies.

Large, tall, wide vase: suits tall stems with fairly large flowers, like round chrysanthemums and phlox.

TABLE SETTINGS

How you set your table depends on how formal an event you want. There are several elements worth considering. Most people never use tablecloths, thinking them a bit dated and formal, but there are many ways of dressing a table without making it look stuffy.

Think about your table in the same way you would the rest of your party. Is there a theme? If it's Christmas, some ivy can work well. If you're having a curry night with friends, visit a sari shop and buy remnants of material to use instead of a tablecloth. For a leaving party for a friend travelling round the world, take some colour photocopies of old maps, stick them on to cork tiles and use them as place mats. You don't have to do anything very fancy – how creative you get with your table settings depends on your abilities.

Even if it's an informal affair, it's still worth bothering to 'dress' your table, however simply, as this will show off your food and drink to its best advantage. And don't forget that if it's a dinner party, your guests will spend most of the evening sat around that table, so it makes sense to spend a bit of time thinking about how it will look.

'A table can be quite intimidating,' says Carl. 'A place setting helps to make an individual area for each person. You can personalise it further by using a small tea light in front of each plate, or use name cards, which are currently very popular for special occasions like birthdays and weddings. You don't have to be creative – you just need to be bold and go for it. If you have a white dinner service, for example, use some coloured rose petals scattered around the outside of the plate to frame it. Or if you have some tiny liqueur glasses, half fill each with water and float a petal on top. Place one in front of each plate. It's just a small touch, won't cost you anything and makes it special.'

If it's an informal dinner with friends, some colour co-ordinated, good quality paper napkins and a few candles is enough to make it feel like you've made an effort. 'There's nothing wrong with paper napkins,' says Carl, 'but go for coloured ones rather than white and try something kitsch if that's the kind of dinner you're having. Don't try and make your paper napkins look like real ones. Just lay them flat. If you're using real napkins, lay them flat or roll them and tie with a piece of ribbon. Don't do origami swans or fans coming out of wine glasses! If you're having a big Sunday brunch, it's better to give people large cloth napkins that they can lay over their laps, or it could get messy.'

Make sure you lay the table in plenty of time and sit down to see it from your guests' point of view. Are the candles or flowers too tall? Will their view of the person opposite them be obscured? Is there enough room for glasses, cutlery, plates, dishes of food, arms, bottles? If you're short of space, keep your table setting simple and uncluttered.

For a smart dinner party, you might want to have a heavy tablecloth as well as proper napkins, but still keep it simple or your guests may feel overwhelmed. I'd really advise you to pull out all the stops only if you have a large table and relatively few guests. Being cramped at dinner for hours will not make for a good night. Of course, if your table feels a bit too big for the amount of people invited, having a more elaborate table setting will help it feel more intimate and cosy. For details of how to lay a place setting for a formal dinner party (where to put which forks, glasses etc.), see Chapter 14.

To be honest, most of the rules about cutlery and glasses being in the right places have gone by the wayside now, except for very formal affairs. Carl says, 'There really are no rules about where to put things. Just do whatever looks good. Lots of people like to mix up their new and old cutlery and crockery now – which is fine and can look good.'

NAME PLACES

If it's a special occasion, it's a good idea to decide where people will sit and put name places at each setting. These don't have to look stuffy as they can be done in an informal, modern style. 'Just scribble a name on a piece of card with pink felt tip pen, or use a silver pen on black card, and tuck into the napkin,' says Carl. 'Don't go down the black calligraphy route! It's dated. Use your imagination and don't be scared. It shows you've put a bit of thought into it and it's just a natural extension to using flowers and candles at a table.'

BUFFET TABLE

If you're throwing a party and have a few dishes on a table, a disposable paper tablecloth is a good idea. Also leave a good supply of paper napkins, cutlery and clean glasses for everyone to help themselves.

USING A CENTREPIECE

Whether you're holding a posh or an informal event, a centrepiece is something that creates a focal point at the table. This could be a small vase of flowers, some candles or even a dish – like a turkey at Christmas, or even a couple of bottles of champagne on ice, waiting to be opened. If you use food or drink as a centrepiece it creates a feeling of anticipation.

DECORATIONS

When it comes to decorating your room/venue that you'll be entertaining in, work with what you have. If there is an unused fireplace in the room, place a large vase of flowers just coming out of the recess. If you have a mantelpiece, use it for candles or trailing tinsel, or hanging streamers. You can use your decorations to emphasise parts of the room or disguise them.

Decorations can be anything – shells you've picked up on your travels, pebbles, marbles in a glass vase, ribbons – as well as the usual pre-packaged streamers, balloons, tinsel, paper chains and paper hanging lanterns. If you have an arty friend who always wraps their Christmas presents beautifully, you can bet they'll be great at decorating a room for a party. Get them to give you a hand on the day, allowing yourselves plenty of time for small emergencies (like running out of drawing pins or Sellotape). Most of your decorating, whether it's the table setting or putting up balloons, can be done well in advance. I'd advise you to do it at least the morning of the event, or preferably the night before. Then you don't have to think of it again.

If you're throwing a children's party you *have to* have some decorations. To ignore this would be like Christmas without a tree. Keep it cheap, cheerful and plentiful. There's nothing worse than a couple of sad balloons hanging in one corner. Kids love bright colours and there are so many 'themed' decoration packs that you can buy, based on their favourite characters, complete with balloons, hats, streamers, napkins and paper plates. (See Chapter 16 on children's party, plus the list of resources at the back for details of suppliers.)

YOUR FURNITURE AND SPACE

If you're having your event at home, think about all the rooms/areas that guests will see and make sure they are ready. For a dancing party or drinks party with several guests, you need to clear as much space as possible. Consider moving furniture out of the room you'll be using. Transform your space by getting rid of items like the TV or hiding your piles of books. If you're hiring a venue, make sure that you understand exactly what furniture you will have on the day and what you won't. If there's anything in there you don't want (like an old piano in the corner) get the banqueting manager to remove it. Some venues sometimes try to do as little as possible to the room they hire out, but it's your prerogative to have it as you want it.

If your event is at home and you have too many chairs, people will sit rather than mingle, so move them to another room. It's good to keep a couple of chairs around so people can sit down when they get a bit weary, and if you're inviting older members of your family, remember that they'll probably want to be sitting most of the time. If you don't have enough chairs, ask a neighbour if you can borrow some, or buy some folding ones. Hiring chairs is expensive and should be avoided unless you are having a very smart event. You may want to remove chairs and place large cushions or a couple of beanbags on the floor to create a less formal feel. Borrow from friends if you can.

To prepare your space for your party/event imagine you are a guest and 'walk through' your home. Start at the front door. What does your porch look like? Are there unemptied dustbins lying around? What will be the first thing your guests see on arrival? Start decorating from your door. Have fun with it. For a children's party, put balloons on the door and a sign with 'PARTY HERE'. For a fancy dress party, stick a mask on your door or a few football scarves if you've got some friends over to watch the FA Cup Final. To make an event really special, trail fairy lights around your front door or, if you have a front garden, along any greenery leading to your door. (Make sure they're suitable for external use, in case it rains.)

Once in the house, think about your hallway and whether there's anything here that could do with a touch of decorating. Clear a space for your guests to leave their coats and bags. Over a bed or an under-stairs cupboard is fine, and make sure you ask a couple of good friends to take people's coats when they come in, in case you're busy. Make sure you check out the toilet and have enough soap and towels to hand. If you're holding a large party, paper hand towels and a large bin are better, as cloth ones will get wet quickly. Put a notice on the toilet door if necessary to let people know where it is.

If any of your guests are smokers, make sure you have a few ashtrays or saucers to hand. You *can't* forbid people to smoke; it makes them feel like social lepers, and anyway, these days most people are sensitive enough to keep it to a minimum and away from the food if they're surrounded by non-smokers. If you really hate smoking that much, don't invite smokers. If you're holding your event in a hired venue, smoking may be forbidden so check beforehand and think about how this will affect the guests you're inviting. You don't want a party where half of your guests are sat on the fire escape all night, puffing away.

YOUR VALUABLES

Lock any rooms you don't want people wandering into, and keep your valuables safe. Put away anything that might be embarrassing – people *do* snoop at parties. A favourite snooping place is the bathroom so check out your cabinet before the event and make sure you don't mind all your guests knowing everything it says about you! Put any valuables or breakables you're concerned about in a cupboard. If you have a computer, and cannot lock a room, place it under the desk and put a long tablecloth over the top. Children in particular are likely to want to 'have a go'.

YOUR FIVE-MINUTE CHECKLIST

→ If you only think about one element of your decor, make it the lighting. Keep it soft and welcoming when you want them to stay, and turn it up when the night is through.

→ Flowers can add colour, disguise bad aspects of a room or draw attention to great ones. Choose the right vase for maximum impact.

→ Keep table settings simple, especially if you're short on space, but do make an effort.

→ 'Walk through' your venue/home as if you were a guest – what needs your attention?

MISTAKES TO AVOID

I WON'T BOTHER WITH THE DECOR – PEOPLE ARE COMING TO SEE ME, AFTER ALL

If you decide to completely bypass all elements of decor, you've really missed a trick. It takes little time to light a few candles or arrange a vase of flowers but they can make a huge difference to the atmosphere of your venue.

I'LL HAVE A HUGE DISPLAY OF FLOWERS ON THE TABLE, THEN THEY WON'T NOTICE THE FOOD TOO MUCH

Beware of going overboard on the decs, especially at the table where – if your guests are seated most of the evening – they can feel intrusive. And don't kid yourself that good decor will make up for bad food or running out of alcohol. It won't. It simply sets the scene.

I FOUND THESE DECORATIONS CHEAP AND, ALTHOUGH THEY'RE REALLY FOR CHRISTMAS, THEY'LL LOOK GREAT FOR OUR HALLOWE'EN PARTY

Stop right there! OK, so there's nothing to stop you using fairy lights all year round or bringing the tinsel out now and again, but if your decorations are *obviously* meant for another season (e.g. they have pictures of Santa on them) then don't use them! You'll ruin the theme of your event and look like a cheapskate to boot.

6 FOOD

I don't know anyone who doesn't like food (and if I did, they'd be no friend of mine). For centuries we've used food to celebrate events, mark special occasions and bring friends and families together. It has huge symbolic meaning and, if you want to get deep about it, represents literal (and metaphorical) sustenance and nurturing.

Food is tied up with many emotions and that's why being invited into someone's house to eat with them is such a wonderful, generous and life-affirming gesture. As a guest it's always flattering to be invited for lunch, brunch or dinner; it shows your host cares and you know you're going to be looked after for the next few hours. Hopefully the company will be great and the event good fun, and you may even get to eat some good food, too. Having a meal with others is as much about the environment and experience as it is about the food itself.

As a host who's decided to entertain friends or family, food is probably the first thing you think about when you know your guests have accepted your invitation. What to buy, cook and serve is crucial to your event. In fact, some hosts only *ever* really think of the food and drink at their events and skip everything else like the planning, decor and music (but you'd never do that, right?).

'They're coming to your house to be entertained by you, but they're not expecting a restaurant-style meal,' says Tony Singh, head chef and co-founder of Scotland's Oloroso restaurant. 'Don't put yourself under too much pressure and do work within your capabilities. Whether it's a dinner party or a picnic, as long as you like what you're making and are happy with it, it'll be fine. Entertaining is about enjoying the company, and this is what people forget. They focus too much on the food. At a good restaurant the food is just part of the experience – the ambience plays a major part.'

WHAT KIND OF FOOD?

In order to decide what kind of food to serve, think about what sort of an event it is. Having a theme or a 'type' of event, like a tea party, a barbecue or a picnic, will help you enormously when it comes to choosing your menu. It's simply easier because your choices are limited by the event itself. (See Chapter 4 for tips on theming.) Be careful of theming around food, though. Nobody wants to eat a blue and green meal. It will look pretty unappetising and you'll have wasted your time. If your event isn't themed, there are so many possibilities when it comes to deciding the menu that you could go round in circles for days. This chapter explains what you need to consider if you want a stress-free ride.

HOW FORMAL IS THIS?

Are you inviting your parents for lunch, the boss round for dinner, or is it just you and the usual gang? Different kinds of foods will be more appropriate for different events. The fancier, more fussed-over the dish looks, the more formal the event will appear. For a formal look, present the meal ready-plated. This means that you dish it up in the kitchen and present it with a bit of thought. So, for example, if you're serving each guest three small lamb chops, pile them overlapping each other, with a sauce around them. People can then help themselves to veg. Unless you're going for a very formal look (and are a great cook) try not to fiddle too much with the food as it can be a bit off-putting to sit down to a meal that's picture perfect.

For a less formal event, take the meal in large dishes onto the dinner table and let everyone pass them round and help themselves. Dessert can be a mound of fresh berries or grapes with some good cheese. The formality of your event will really determine what you cook. If making an excellent impression is vital and you're really not up to it, consider getting some outside help in. Some caterers will cook in your kitchen then leave you to dish up. (See the Resources chapter at the end for details, plus Chapter 11 on hiring professionals.) Or better still, opt for a drinks party instead where the food will be limited to nibbles that you can buy in from your local deli or have delivered.

WHAT'S YOUR BUDGET?

Yes, you really need to think about this. How much would you like to spend on this event? Before you rush off to the supermarket, think about how many guests you have coming and do a rough costing of the meal. It's easy to get carried away and end up spending a small fortune when you were originally planning modest, simple fare. If you find your costs look like they're spiralling out of control, don't panic. There's usually an easy way of cutting back.

Avoid using red meat – fish and chicken are far less expensive and with the trend towards healthier eating, many people prefer them. Think about buying one of the courses ready-made, such as the dessert. If you have none of the ingredients at home to make your dessert, you'll have to buy them all from scratch and that will end up costing you more.

Consider whether you really need three courses. Life is a lot less formal these days and few people have any firm expectations when they go to someone's house for a meal. Most of us are happy with a few nibbles with our first drink while the food is cooking, a main course and a dessert.

BUFFET FOOD

If you're holding a buffet-type event, spread the food out as much as possible along your table. If it's a large buffet, have the same dishes at different ends of the table to prevent a bottleneck of guests down one end, or someone hogging the best dish. After about fifteen minutes, the buffet table will look wrecked so don't fuss over whether the food is well presented. Chances are this is a less formal event anyway.

Concentrate on using pretty dishes for your food, the table setting and other decorations. Clear away any empty dishes as you go along if you have time, but don't worry too much about it. (Never start washing up halfway through a party!) As far as what to cook is concerned, you can always ask others to help by bringing along a dish each (though specify what kind of dish you'd like, so you don't end up with five pasta salads). Avoid anything with mayonnaise or fish as, left standing for hours, it won't look too good and could pose a health risk.

Of course the lesson here is to have a budget at the outset. For details of how to go about it, see Chapter 3. And if you think you're too cool to budget anything, think again. It isn't as nerdy as it sounds and it'll save you time, money and hassle in the long run. Promise.

HOW MUCH TIME DO YOU HAVE?

A vital question that any good host always considers. If you have a busy lifestyle, don't make life harder by leaving everything to the last minute. Make sure you plan your event ahead of time, allow lots of time for food shopping (at the very least, the day before), maybe even choose a meal that can be prepared a day or so in advance.

Before I plan a meal for friends, I always think about what I'm doing a few days beforehand and how busy (and tired) I'm likely to be. If you decide to prepare a three-course meal on a Friday night after a hard week at work, you're either superhuman or a masochist. Remember that the point isn't to impress everyone with your Michelin-starred efforts. The point is to create an event your guests (and you) thoroughly enjoy.

GETTING PREPARATION DONE

The other consideration is how much of your menu is 'last minute' – i.e. needs to be done then and there. Avoid anything fiddly or that requires lots of last-minute attention, as you'll want to mix with your guests rather than spend half an hour in the kitchen. The more you can prepare beforehand the better. Chefs do this all the time, cooking practically everything on the day or the day before then just heating it up to serve it. This sounds horrible but it really isn't. I guarantee that 80 per cent of the lovely meals you've eaten in restaurants are cooked in this way. (Do you *really* think they make everything from scratch on demand?)

Tony Singh says, 'At a restaurant, everything is done to a certain stage beforehand. The more expensive the restaurant the less is pre-prepared because they have got the staff to finish it off then and there. At home, it's just you so get it prepared. Use steamers to heat up veg that has already been blanched [plunged in boiling water for a couple of minutes then refreshed in cold]. As you become more experienced, you'll get to know what you're comfortable with leaving till the last minute and what you're not. Try not to leave too much till the last minute.'

If you use your common sense and make sure everything is stored carefully, it can work very well. I wouldn't cook fish the day before but of course, a clever cook doesn't serve fish if they want a dish that can stand reheating. I have a friend who is a great host, and she prepares the lot beforehand, carefully choosing dishes that she knows she can cook early. She's even been known to cook mash the day before. Then she puts everything in the oven to heat on the day. If you choose your menu carefully you can do this, too.

HOW GOOD A COOK ARE YOU?

The one mistake people make time and again when entertaining is they either try a new dish on their guests (uh-oh) or they try something far too complicated. You don't have to be a cordon bleu chef to entertain – even someone with modest skills, a bit of imagination and time can throw together a great meal. The trick is to know your limitations.

'A very basic rule, but the first thing I'd say to anyone, is to keep it simple,' says Terry Farr, winner of several awards and chef patron of Friends restaurant in Pinner, England. 'The secret of our success – and many good restaurants' – is that although it looks good on the plate and tastes great, we keep it simple. Sometimes people over-elaborate on things. And the more you do that, the more chance you have of things going wrong.'

When you do fancy experimenting with food, do it when you have no guests. Don't expect to pull off a new recipe first time. World-class chefs take several attempts to perfect their recipes, testing and tasting again and again. If you do the same you will improve quickly. Everyone needs to rehearse and it really is true that where cooking is concerned, lots of practice gives you confidence and skill. Someone once told me that whenever I had guests for dinner, I underwent an extreme personality change in the kitchen, because I'd get so stressed in case something went wrong. Several years on, I've got more confident and relaxed by practising and using recipes I know well (as well as lightening up a bit). I no longer do a Jekyll and Hyde act in the kitchen.

Remember that food is not the only reason your guests have come. They want to enjoy the whole evening. If you stress over the food (or any aspect of your event) your guests will pick up on this, feel guilty and won't enjoy themselves as much.

SHOPPING FOR INGREDIENTS

When shopping for ingredients, the first rule is to buy the best you can afford. Quality is crucial. The better your ingredients are, the less you'll need to do to them and the less important your cooking skills will be. Who needs to know how to cook when you can serve a starter of buffalo mozzarella salad with vine-ripened plum tomatoes on a big platter? Add some freshly baked ciabatta from the local deli and you've pulled off a fantastic first course, with minimum effort. Try the same thing with watery, tasteless tomatoes or a rock hard French stick and, well, you get the idea.

The more you shop for ingredients, the more confident you'll become at spotting what's good and what isn't. Use your eyes and nose when it comes to fresh produce. Does it look like it's fresh today? Don't be embarrassed to ask. See if you can have a small taste or a sniff. What's your gut instinct? If something looks like it's been sitting around for days, it probably has.

Supermarkets are, of course, highly convenient for most of us. They do, however, make huge demands on their suppliers, even stating what shape and size the fruit/veg has to be before they buy it. The result is that their offerings are homogenised and can sometimes lack real flavour. Also, they often pick crops well before they're ripe, refrigerate them to keep them that way, then put them on their shelves to ripen. You don't need me to tell you that a tomato that's ripened in the sun is going to taste better than one that's ripened under fluorescent lights.

If you have the time, try buying at least some of your ingredients from specialist shops (butchers, bakers, fishmongers). You'll get a better choice of fish from a fishmonger and often it will have been caught that day. Tip: don't buy fish on a Monday as it most certainly *wasn't* caught at the weekend! (And for the same reason don't order it in a restaurant on a Monday, either.)

The second rule of food shopping is to buy what's in season and, if possible, something that's locally produced. If you don't know what's in season, ask. You'll get the freshest, best produce that way and it won't have made a long plane journey to get to you. Of course this isn't always possible, but it's worth keeping in mind that the seasons are important to most good chefs and they tend to plan their menus around them. In fact, if you have time, visit the shops and see what's available before deciding what to make. You never know, you may even be inspired. Other places to shop are local markets, farmers' markets (where people bring their own produce, often organic) and at delicatessens.

HOW MUCH TO COOK

Some people like to cook exactly the right amount and have nothing left over when entertaining, but it's so difficult to judge how to do this. How do you know how hungry your guests are going to be, or which dishes they'll want seconds of? I'm of the opinion that it's better to cook a bit too much than not enough. If you have a little left over, it doesn't matter (and most things taste better the next day, anyway, eaten cold for breakfast with a hangover – don't tell me you've never done that). However, if you run out of food it's embarrassing, unless you're amongst very good friends. Food equals hospitality. When it runs out, it looks like your hospitality has too. If food runs out after everyone's had their fill, that's fine. But if you misjudge quantities and don't cook enough in the first place, guests will feel uneasy about tucking in if they can see that supplies are running out.

If you're worried whether you've cooked enough, offer to dish up for everyone and give them modest amounts. If you have time, buy some fresh bread, such as focaccia or ciabatta, and place a basket of it on the table. 'If there's not enough food it can be deadly,' say Maria Hipwell and Liz Ellerton, founders of Lilies and Chips, a company that creates bespoke party themes and invitations. 'If you're having a party from, say, 7–11 p.m., hold back some of the food and bring it out at around 9 p.m. Otherwise, your guests may leave to get pizza.'

Don't go the other way, however, and cook too much. Terry says, 'People always prepare too much – it seems we can't get our head round what's enough. When I go to relatives' houses for Sunday lunch they always have so many vegetables – bowl after bowl after bowl. I think to myself, why didn't you just do two or three nice green vegetables and keep it simple?

'These days, guests would rather eat something well-cooked and a reasonable portion, than have food piled high on their plates. Weigh out your basic ingredients. A rough guide is about 4oz (113g) of meat per person – so for ten guests that works out at 40oz, about 2½ pounds (1.1kg). That's enough. Some people will end up cooking 6–8 pounds of chicken! For veg, again, you need a maximum of 6oz (170g). If you have three types of veg, that's 2oz (approximately 60g) of each. Weigh it before it's peeled and cooked. If you stick to these guidelines, you won't run out, don't worry.

'This is how we do it when we cater for functions. If you're cooking for a hundred people, you can't afford to over-cater and you have to have enough. Meat is filling and people can only eat a certain amount. When my youngest brother got married, it was just him and his new wife at home for their first Christmas. They bought a 17lb turkey. We still laugh about it now!'

With practice, you'll be able to judge how much to cook. Quantities that are particularly difficult to get right are pasta, rice and couscous, because they all swell with cooking and are very filling. I nearly always end up making far too much, even when I think I've got a modest amount. Follow a recipe if you are concerned about quantities. Tip: potatoes always run out, salad never does. For amounts to cook when catering for a party, see below.

BALANCING YOUR MENU

Think about the time of year and weather. If the country's in the middle of a heat wave, you won't want to have a hot soup starter or cook something heavy. Fruit or ice cream are perfect for summer desserts. In the dead of winter, people love homely, hot dishes. The balance of colours, textures and tastes is important, too, when planning a meal. Think about the entirety – if you are having a fish main course, do you really want fish for starter, too? If you and all your guests adore fish, fine. If you're having a goat's cheese salad starter, don't opt for a creamy dessert.

Imagine eating your way through the complete menu and think about how you'll feel at the end of the meal. You want to leave your guests happily satisfied but not stuffed and feeling sickly. When compiling your menu, it's better to err on the side of making it light, as then your guests will appreciate the dessert and will want coffee, too. If you stuff them to the gills, they'll probably feel sluggish and the evening will take on the same feel. The easiest way to plan a meal is to think about your main course first, as that's the star attraction, and build the rest of the menu around that.

CAN'T VEGETARIANS JUST EAT THE SALAD?

In a word, no. If you invite people to dinner you must cater for their dietary needs. When your guests RSVP, ask them if there is anything they don't like or can't eat. The last thing you want is to be caught unawares on the day, when someone announces, 'Oh I'm vegetarian, now, didn't you know?' If any of your guests *are* veggie you will have to accept it with good grace and make something for them.

An easy way out is to have a vegetarian menu that everyone eats, then you don't have to make something special. But please don't think that you can get away with just giving them extra potatoes, salad or an omelette. As an ex-veggie I can tell you nothing is worse than being invited to someone's house for dinner and finding out that all you can eat are the accompaniments. And don't forget to find out what your guests mean by 'vegetarian' as many people use that term now when they actually eat fish, too. If you're serving anything with cheese in it, make sure it is suitable for vegetarians (i.e. not made with animal rennet). It will say on the pack.

You may find that some of your guests have food intolerances, avoid certain foods or are on an elimination diet. Some people do this because they have a genuine health problem that's exacerbated by certain foods, whilst others do it through choice. Common food culprits are cows' milk, wheat and dairy. And, of course, if your guests are allergic to anything they need to let you know, as an allergic reaction to food is probably the worst thing that can happen at a dinner party. As host, it's up to you to put your guests at ease, so don't make them feel that their dietary requirements are a pain – even if they are. Never show that you've been put out. It's just bad manners.

FEEDING CHILDREN

Kids can be tricky to feed because many of them have very definite likes and dislikes. In the likes category often go pizza, chips, chicken, potatoes, pasta. In the dislike category, any fruit or veg. This of course is a generalisation but it's amazing how many children do have these tastes. When entertaining children you must cater to their tastes. Ask them (or their parents) beforehand what they will and won't eat. Many teenagers are veggie so check this out, too. This is also a great time to make more food than you think you may need, as children seem to have an incredible ability for hoovering up huge quantities, especially teenagers who are going through a growth spurt.

BUYING READY-MADE

If it's an informal, mid-week supper there is nothing wrong with buying ready-made food to serve to guests, as long as you choose wisely. Most supermarkets have a 'premium' ready-made range that boasts the kind of food you'd find in smart restaurants. Delis and gourmet shops are also a great source of ready-made food that can be heated and served. If your cooking abilities are limited and/or time is short, ready-made food can be a godsend.

Obviously, if your event is fairly formal, it's up to you to judge whether you can pull it off. One way to do this is to buy the main course ready-made – say parma-wrapped chicken breast – and make the accompaniments, like parmesan mash and spinach. Customise ready-made food and your guests really won't feel like they're eating packet meals. Don't forget that presentation is particularly important if serving something ready-made. And of course you do *not* serve it in the tin foil dish it comes in. But you don't need me to tell you that, do you?

If pride means you'd rather not resort to 'packet food', but you still need help, try your local deli where they will have the same kind of fare but probably prepared that day. Some of the most exclusive parties are 'catered for', which is just another way of saying that someone else has done the cooking. Of course, whether you tell your guests that it's ready-made or pretend you've done it all yourself is up to you and your conscience.

SHORTCUTS TO CHEATING WITH STYLE

→ Warm bread in the oven before serving for a 'fresh-baked' taste and aroma. If it's crusty, wrap in foil first to prevent it going hard.

→ Buy frozen bread rolls and bake them to serve with the main course.

→ Use fresh herbs to garnish meals and make them look more appealing. Look on the packs to see which herb goes with which food.

→ Float a swirl of single cream on top of shop-bought fresh soup for that home-made look.

→ Buy ready-peeled veg and ready washed salad to save time. More expensive but worth it if you're busy.

→ Celebrity chefs always tell us how easy it is to make fresh stock and freeze it. I say, get a life. You can buy good quality fresh stock that's in the chiller cabinet. Or get a bottle of the stuff you can add boiling water to for 'instant' stock. Unless, of course, you like the idea of boiling bones and stuff for hours, to make your own.

→ Tony Singh says, 'Pile food into large dishes and place on the table for people to help themselves. Don't feel you have to present it like restaurant food.'

FOOD FOR PARTIES

If you're having a drinks party, you still have to supply *some* food. Otherwise your guests will probably get very drunk, very quickly. Deciding how much food to supply and what kind depends on the kind of party you're having. If it's likely to get pretty crowded and rowdy, and you want people to dance and really chill out, some crisps, cocktail sausages, nibbles and a few dips with crudités is probably enough. Mini chocolates always go down well towards the end of the evening.

People understand that they haven't come to eat, and most will have eaten beforehand. This is why it's important to let guests know when you invite them what kind of party you're holding.

If you're having a smart cocktail party, have posher nibbles like hand-cooked crisps, or canapés, like blinis topped with cream cheese and smoked salmon and crostini. Allow about eight canapés per person and don't make more than four things. Prepare all the food beforehand and don't have anything that needs cooking. Mixing cocktails will take up most of your time.

With both kinds of parties, stick to finger food only (no plates, no washing up) and don't have anything that will result in debris – like olive stones, bits of prawn shells and so on. Keep it simple. If you want people to move from room to room, it's a good idea to place food at various points so everyone doesn't crowd around one table. If your event is a formal one, seriously consider calling in the professionals. They can arrive with ready-cooked nibbles and can even provide waiting staff to hand food round and serve drinks.

Unless you are a very good cook who is highly organised and has lots of time, don't even contemplate catering for hoards of people by yourself at a formal function. There are too many things that can go wrong and, even if they all go right, you will exhaust yourself. If you're really determined to do it yourself, make the numbers smaller and prepare it all beforehand so people can just help themselves and you don't have to spend all evening in the kitchen bobbing your head in and out of the oven.

HOW DO I MAKE SURE IT'S ALL READY AT THE SAME TIME?

Plan, plan, plan. The easiest way to make sure that all the components of your meal are ready at the same time (and on time), is to have a schedule and work backwards. First decide what time you want to eat. Then work backwards to see what time you need to do everything else. Of course, getting everything on the table at the same time is particularly important if you're serving hot food. There's nothing worse than lukewarm vegetables accompanied by sizzling chicken. Even experienced cooks work from a timetable as it's by far the best way of making sure it's all hot at the same time.

A simple example of a timetable

To eat the main course at 8 p.m.:

Chicken in oven at 6.30 p.m.

Potatoes in oven at 7 p.m.

Bread in oven at 7.45 p.m.

Heat gravy at 7.50 p.m.

Veg on at 7.50 p.m.

Extras: lemon wedges/herbs

Obviously the more courses, the more complicated the timetable. Writing it all down like this will also help you remember everything. Add on the end of your timetable any garnishes/extras that must also be added at the last minute. I tend to invite guests around 45 minutes before I want to serve dinner. That gives them 15 minutes to be late and half an hour to have a drink and be introduced to other guests beforehand. Don't ask people to come at 8 p.m. expecting them to sit down then and eat straight away. Very few people ever arrive dead on time, and it's much more relaxed to feel that you can have a drink and a chat first.

For more detailed advice, see Chapters 12–19, which focus on various, specific events from how to throw a dinner party to planning a wedding reception.

IF THE WORST HAPPENS

You drop the food on the floor; you forget to turn the oven on; you burn the dinner – take your pick. If the worst really happens, try to relax and not get too stressed. Tell your guests (with humour rather than anger!) that you've had a mishap and suggest phoning for a take-out. Of course, you should pay for the meal. Most people will be sympathetic and, if you seem to be quite relaxed about it all, will probably find it funny. They will take their lead from you, though, so if they hear you sobbing in the kitchen chances are you won't see them for dust.

YOUR FIVE-MINUTE CHECKLIST

→ Buy the freshest, best, seasonal ingredients you can and do as little as possible to them.

→ Prepare everything as far ahead as possible. Leave very little to do on the actual day.

→ Know your limits when cooking and test out a new recipe on a good friend first before unleashing it on the world. Never cook something you haven't tried before, successfully.

→ Keep it simple, easy and present it well.

→ Taste it before you serve it. Tony says, 'This is one of the biggest mistakes people make – they don't taste as they go along. Good chefs would never serve something they hadn't tasted first.'

→ Remember that food is to be enjoyed. Have fun with it.

→ Work out your timetable so that everything is ready at the same time.

MISTAKES TO AVOID

IT'S NOTHING SPECIAL, I'LL DO THE SHOPPING AN HOUR BEFOREHAND

Big mistake. You will find that the store has run out of the one essential ingredient you need (the fish for your fish pie!) and that you have to rethink your menu at the eleventh hour. Even if your event is informal, you should still make the effort to plan.

I CAN'T BE BOTHERED WITH RECIPES – I'LL MAKE IT UP AS I GO ALONG

Very few people can get away with this. Intuitive cooking is for those who have been cooking for years and really know what they're doing. That doesn't mean that you can't add a twist of your own here and there, but be careful with quantities as recipes are carefully tested several times for a reason.

I'LL JUST DOUBLE THE QUANTITIES TO MAKE TWICE AS MUCH

This can work for some recipes (and they usually say in them if that's the case). For others, it's a disaster. If a recipe has a lot of a particular flavour in it – herbs, spices, garlic or lemons – unless it tells you it's OK to double the quantities, then don't. It will be too overpowering and probably ruin the dish. Add just a touch more than it says in the recipe as these flavours go a long way. If you're doubling a quantity of rice, couscous or pasta, make sure the liquid it's cooking in is doubled too.

7 DRINK

There's nothing nicer than walking into someone's house, or turning up at a function, and being offered that first drink. A glass of something on arrival, whether alcoholic or not, always goes down well. From an ice-cold glass of Pimms on a sweltering hot day, to a freshly brewed cup of tea after a long, winter's walk, a welcoming drink is always warmly received. It's a way of greeting your guests and showing that you're pleased to see them. It also marks the beginning of what will be, hopefully, an enjoyable, sociable day/evening.

For centuries, drink has been used to oil the wheels of social gatherings – to toast people's health, make announcements and generally get the show on the road. Two mistakes people often make with drink when entertaining (especially where serving wine is concerned) is that they either pay too much attention to it or not enough. By that I mean that they either get far too hung up on which wine goes with which food, putting themselves under pressure to impress and feeling intimated in case they make a 'mistake'. Or they treat it as an afterthought, and more or less just serve up any old thing.

SO HOW IMPORTANT IS IT?

Whatever your event – picnic, barbecue, kids' party, romantic dinner for two – you need to provide drink of some kind. What you serve, how much of it and the cost will depend on the kind of gathering you're having. Obviously at a cocktail party, the drinks need more thought and planning than they would at a dinner party because they're the star attraction. But don't be fooled into thinking that just because you've taken time to create a great meal for half a dozen friends, you don't need to think about the drink. You do.

Throwing a great event means paying attention to every aspect of the evening, and the best hosts are the ones who do just that. Why go to all that bother of deciding on your menu – balancing tastes, and making sure your courses all work well together – and then just add any drink that comes to hand?

WHAT TO BUY AND HOW MUCH

Evening event: unless all your guests are teetotal (or underage), Western society deems it the civilised thing to offer alcohol with any evening meal you're serving.

Daytime event: many people probably won't want to drink alcohol (though it is nice to be given the choice). Daytime drinking can make you feel sluggish, so people often choose to limit their intake.

Children's party: obviously you'll be serving soft drinks for the children, and you may want to offer their parents a glass of something alcoholic. Keep the alcohol limited (a glass or two at the most is plenty, as these events are bound to be daytime, too). Also, this is not the time for guests to get tipsy. And, of course, it goes without saying that any alcohol on offer should be kept well away from children's reach!

Summer daytime events: the heat has a dehydrating effect on us all. Keep this in mind if preparing a barbecue or picnic. Make sure you have plenty of ice and long, non-alcoholic drinks on offer (for example, cranberry juice, soda with lime, sparkling water with lemon slices and fresh mint). Alcohol will affect everyone more in the heat (i.e. we become drunker, faster) so you may want to focus more on non- or low-alcohol alternatives. For picnics, try wine-in-a-box – there's more choice than there used to be and it's easier than transporting bottles.

Formal celebrations: if you're planning a wedding reception, for example, then a glass of champagne for each guest to toast the newlyweds is a must. If your budget is tight, try a cheaper, fizzy alternative such as Cava which is very drinkable and (unless all your guests are champagne snobs) really very good.

With *every* event, day or night: provide non-alcoholic alternatives. There are a number of reasons a guest may not want to drink, and they shouldn't have to explain to you, or anyone, why they may be abstaining. Apart from the obvious – e.g. they're the designated driver for the evening, or they simply don't like drinking – they may have highly personal reasons that they don't want to discuss. Be sensitive to this. They could be recovering alcoholics, or undergoing medical treatment that rules out alcohol. Don't put them under pressure. Your job as host is to make everyone feel at ease. Always provide three non-alcoholic choices (so it really *is* a choice, and not just a case of orange juice or water).

RUNNING OUT OF DRINK

We place so much emphasis on drink in our society, and the amount of alcohol drunk is often mistakenly linked to how much fun we're having. Therefore, every host's nightmare is that they will run out of alcohol (and their event will become an unmitigated disaster).

By all means buy more drink than you feasibly need, but remember that the success of your event isn't reliant on how much your guests can drink. And running out of drink is not the end of the world. That's what late-night stores and off-licences are for. If there isn't one nearby, then you will just have to start drinking something else in the house. Unless you are hosting a formal event (in which case experts can help you calculate how much to buy) running out of drink is not nearly the disaster everyone thinks it is. That said, of course it's preferable not to run out.

WHAT TO CONSIDER WHEN BUYING YOUR DRINK

→ A lot depends on your guests. Who have you invited and are they big drinkers? Think about other events you've attended with them – what was their drinking 'behaviour'?

→ What time of day is your event? (People always drink more in the evening than during the day.)

→ What day is your event? Weekdays (when most of us have to get up to go to work the next day) tend to find people limiting their alcohol, as do Sundays. On Friday or Saturday nights, however, most of us have that end-of-the-week feeling and are likely to drink more.

→ What life stage are your friends at? If they're younger and don't have children, chances are they'll be more up for a 'big night'. If your guests are exhausted parents who have to get up early to watch their son play football in the park, they probably won't. Students in their late teens/early 20s are notoriously big drinkers. It seems to go with the territory. Of course this is all a generalisation, but it tends to be fairly accurate.

→ And finally (but most importantly) what kind of an event is it? People drink more alcohol when it's accompanied by food. If you're throwing a dinner party, your guests will drink more as the event lasts several hours. At a drinks or dancing party, guests will pace themselves as you'll probably only have nibbles on offer or a small buffet at the most. The exception, of course, is New Year's Eve; it seems that most of us are willing to see in the New Year with the mother of all hangovers.

HOW MUCH TO BUY

These are rough estimates only, for those who feel they need them. Nobody knows your guests better than you do, so it's just as important to look at the list of questions above and go with your gut feeling.

Dinner party: approximately one bottle of wine per person. Buy better quality wine for a dinner party than a drinks party. If possible, spend about twice what you would normally pay for a bottle of everyday wine that you might drink at home.

Evening drinks party: approximately half a bottle of wine per person.

Daytime party: approximately one third of a bottle of wine per person.

And don't forget:

→ Plenty of ice – especially in the summer, or if you have a small fridge and don't have space to chill all your drink.
→ Water (still and sparkling).
→ A good choice of non-alcoholic beverages (including non-fizzy options like home-made lemonade or cranberry juice).

WHERE TO BUY DRINK

If you're buying for a large event, the best place to buy from is a store that allows you to return any unopened bottles. You buy more wine than you will need, then you return the extra, immediately after your event, and get a refund. This service doesn't cost you anything, and most reputable wine merchants and off-licences are more than happy to oblige, even on relatively small amounts (i.e. a case or two). These stores usually hire out glasses, too, and also sell ice.

Visiting a wine warehouse (such as Majestic in the UK) is also a good idea as the range there is enormous and the staff are highly knowledgeable. (See the Resources chapter for details.)

Warehouses also allow tastings, so if something takes your fancy but you're unsure if you'll like it, ask for a taste. I'd advise buying your wine after you've decided on the food you're serving, as then you can match it to the flavours of the meal.

GET EXPERT HELP

If you know very little about wine, it really doesn't matter. There are many ways you can learn (see below). And anyway, that's what the staff are there for. Many off-licences and wine merchants boast knowledgeable staff who can help you decide what to buy. Also, in recent years, wine labels have become more informative and this can help you choose the variety that's right for you.

Supermarkets are now stocking a wider range of wines than ever before. Although not all their staff will have a decent knowledge of wine, there's usually one person instore who knows what they're talking about. Get to know them and ask for them by name next time.

GUESTS CONTRIBUTING

When invited to dinner, or a party, most guests will ask 'can I bring anything?' Don't be shy. Ask for whatever would help, whether it's a bottle of wine or the dessert course. I always ask guests who drink very little to bring a non-alcoholic drink that they like. That way, that's one less thing to worry about. Most guests will turn up at a dinner party with a bottle of something. Don't feel obliged to open it if you don't want to, or if it doesn't match your food well. Of course, the better you know your guests the more specific you can be. There's no reason why you can't ask a good friend to bring along a bottle of wine that goes well with a specific course, say, a bottle of Sauvignon Blanc for the goat's cheese salad you're serving as a starter.

CAN I ASK GUESTS TO PAY FOR THEIR DRINKS?

Not in your own house, no! But if your event is being held in a formal venue, you can. Make it clear when you invite them that you've put a certain amount of money behind the bar, then after that it will be a 'pay bar'. You can word the invitation something along the lines of: 'Free bar till 9 p.m., then pay bar will operate'. People don't mind contributing, as they understand that entertaining can be very expensive. But if they're expected to dig into their pockets, do let them know before they arrive, so there are no nasty surprises!

MATCHING WINE TO FOOD

OK, this is the biggie. People seem to tie themselves up in knots when it comes to choosing which wine should go with which food. Yes, there are some basic 'rules', but the bottom line is to use them as a general guide and go with what you like. Of course, there are some wines that will make your food taste even better and some that will be a bit of a disaster pairing, but at the end of the day it really is up to you. As with every other element of entertaining, I'd advise you to approach choosing wine with a sense of fun, enjoy it and just don't take the whole thing too seriously. There's nothing worse than a host who's a wine bore.

Fiona Sims, a food and wine expert and author of *Guide to Wine* (Parragon, 2001) says, 'Things have changed. Sticking to Chablis with fish, claret with beef – those days have gone. There's nothing wrong with Chablis and fish, but there's a whole new world of wine out there and better matches to be made.'

ASK FOR HELP

Use the expert advice on offer (see above), visit the websites listed in the Resources chapter for a crash course on which foods go with which wines, or enlist the help of a knowledgeable friend. Tell them what you're cooking and ask for some advice. People love to feel needed and they'll be only too happy to help.

WHAT WORKS WITH WHAT

You know one rule when it comes to serving wine, right? White with white meat and red with red meat. Well forget that. The wine world seems to have loosened up over the past decade – it's now deemed OK to serve red wine with fish. But with more now on offer – Australian, Chilean, Kiwi, Italian, French, German, South African and even English wine – the choice seems more confusing than ever.

HERE'S FIONA SIMS' SIMPLE GUIDE TO CHOOSING WINE

→ The first thing to think about is the **flavour** of the dish you're cooking. The bolder the flavour of the dish, the bolder the wine must be to stand up to it. There's no point pairing a light Grenache with a rich venison stew – it simply won't stand up. Try a red Bandol instead. And if you'd like to serve more than one wine at a meal, start with the dryer ones and move on to the sweet.

→ Also think about any **sauce** in your meal, as this too will have an effect on which wine works best. If you're steaming a meal, you'll need to try something light so you don't obliterate the taste. If it has a deep, meaty sauce, a punchier wine will work well.

→ **Acidity** is also important. If you have a fatty meal – such as duck – choose a wine with a bit of acidity, such as Pinot Noir, to cut through the fat.

→ With **sweet food**, your wine needs to be equally sweet, if not more so. Though there are some famous exceptions that work well, like Stilton and port.

BEST AND WORST MATCHES

There are some wines that work exceptionally well together, and some that are a disaster. Here, wine expert Fiona Sims gives a run-down of the best and worst matches to look out for.

FIVE MATCHES MADE IN HEAVEN

Parmesan and sweet oloroso

Goats' cheese and Sauvignon Blanc

Pasta with sausage sauce and Dolcetto

Roast lamb and Ribera del Duero

Mussels and Muscadet

FIVE MATCHES MADE IN HELL

Yoghurt and Chardonnay

Skate and capers with Zinfandel

Asparagus and Merlot

Artichokes and oaked Sémillon

Peppered steak and Cabernet Sauvignon

(You may also like to look at the following website for good advice on matching foods with wine: **www.bbr.com**)

ROUGH GUIDE TO SERVING WINE

Glasses: obvious, I know, but use wine glasses for wine. These tend to be tulip-shaped or curve inwards. The reason? They allow you to swirl the wine round and get a whiff of its lovely bouquet. Also, the shape of the glass determines where the wine lands on your tongue – and which taste buds it stimulates first. Wine buffs never fill a glass more than a third full as this allows the air to get to it and helps you appreciate its aroma.

Temperature: there are no real strict rules here – it may depend on what your personal preference is – but the general belief is that white wine should be colder than red. That said, chilling a wine does change its taste slightly, so if you've spent a lot of money on a white wine, it's best to under-chill it than over-chill, so you can get the full benefit of the flavour. The best way to chill a wine is to put ice and water in an ice bucket – though I have to admit I tend to shove it in the freezer at the last minute! Chiller jackets that are permanently in the freezer compartment and can be slipped onto a bottle of wine are very useful (though admittedly don't look very elegant). Of course, aesthetically a chrome ice bucket wins hands down every time.

Chill white wine to around 7–9°C (45–48°F) and red to 15–18°C (60–64°F), though if they're fruitier reds they taste better a little chilled.

At the end of the day, temperature is really up to you. In Cyprus I drank copious amounts of the very good, local red wine with ice. Here, it just doesn't taste the same.

Decanting: the idea of decanting a wine into a glass flagon seems a bit old-fashioned these days, though it's a useful way of getting rid of the sediment from a mature wine. (As you see the sediment rise to the neck of the wine bottle, stop pouring.) If you do have a mature wine you want to drink and think there may be sediment in the bottom, make sure you keep the bottle standing for a day or two before uncorking. When wine is exposed to the air, it accelerates the maturing process, that's why old wine needs to be drunk quickly once decanted. Young, tannic red wine is sometimes decanted to help it mature more quickly. Wine like this can taste better if allowed to stand in a decanter for a while.

I have to admit I've never decanted a bottle of wine in my life and don't think that it's really necessary.

Presenting soft drinks: however, I do think it's worth 'decanting' soft drinks, or pouring them into pretty vases and adding ice cubes and perhaps some decoration (fresh berries or mint leaves), along with a couple of cocktail swizzles for stirring. Much nicer than having a carton of supermarket orange juice on the dinner table. Also, anyone not drinking alcohol still wants to feel special. If you're serving them something fizzy (like soda water and lime), consider using a cocktail glass or champagne flute, rather than a big, clumsy tumbler that makes them feel like a toddler at the grown-ups' table.

What's a 'corked' wine? There's more 'corked' or 'off' wine out there than you might think. You might notice a horrible, mouldy smell, which is caused by fungus contaminating the cork during the bottling process. If this happens, the wine itself will take on the same aroma and taste 'off'. It's estimated that around 1 in 20 bottles of wine are 'corked', perhaps more. That's why plastic corks have been developed. If you find a corked wine, take it back to the wine merchant or send it back in a restaurant. It happens. (Another reason it's worth tasting a wine before serving it, and having a bottle or two extra in case the worst happens.)

Vinegar taste: this is due to the wine being exposed to too much air and oxidising. If storing half-drunk wine, get a vacuum pump that gets rid of the air and keeps the wine drinkable for the next day or so. A vinegar taste can also happen when the cork has dried out (that's why wine is stored on its side, especially if kept for long periods).

White crystals: if you see these deposits at the bottom of your bottle, don't worry. They're called tartrates and are natural deposits that come from the tartaric acid in the wine. You'll be pleased to hear that they don't affect the wine or its drinkability.

Should wine 'breathe'? Not really. It doesn't make much difference if you uncork it an hour or two before serving or directly before.

AT THE TABLE

→ Make sure you have at least one corkscrew available if not two. There are various types and it depends on which you find the easiest, though I think the more state-of-the-art they are the less effective they seem to be. Wine waiters prefer a lever version that is twisted into the cork then pulled out by levering a metal hinge against the neck of the bottle. A practically foolproof corkscrew has to be the one with arms that go up as you twist it into the cork. Pull the arms down and you're done.

→ If you are entertaining six or more people, place identical bottles of wine at each end of the table so it's within easy reach of everyone. The same goes for any jugs of soft drinks or water that you're serving.

GETTING READY FOR A BIG PARTY

→ Get your drink in the day before the event, so you can work out where to put it. If you don't have a large fridge, get a cold box ready for chilling. Failing that, use a bath or cleaned out large plastic bin (obviously only for informal affairs!). You can buy ice from supermarkets or off-licences.

→ The day before, don those rubber gloves, rinse all glasses in very hot water and let them dry naturally (right way up). Polish off with a clean tea towel if necessary before the party starts. Don't use detergent on glasses as this can affect the taste of the drink. Very hot water should do the trick.

→ Open bottles of wine beforehand to save time. Enlist the help of a friend to serve drinks on guests' arrival. If you're serving champagne (or something fizzy) don't pre-open it or it will go flat.

→ Have all your garnishes prepared – olives, lemon/lime slices – as well as ice in a bucket, serviettes (if serving finger food) and some clean napkins for those inevitable spills. (See Chapter 12 for more tips on preparing for a drinks party.)

LEARNING MORE ABOUT WINE

As well as tapping into the knowledge of the staff at your local wine merchants, there are other ways of learning about wine. Ask at your local off-licence about wine tasting events or courses or see your local library. Also, check out the Resources chapter at the end of this book for information on where to go to learn more. There are even wine clubs you can join online.

If you and your friends are interested in wine, why not have a wine tasting party? You can take it as seriously (or not) as you want. Ask each guest to arrive with a bottle or two of something 'interesting', pour the wine into several glasses and get each guest to taste it at the same time and comment on what they think. (A bit like a reading group, but a lot less work!) And once you build up your knowledge, you could even do blind tastings and see if you can guess what the wine is. There are many books on the market that explain how to 'taste' wine.

THE ORDER OF DRINKS

At a fairly formal function, the order of drinking goes as follows:

An aperitif – this is to whet the appetite and can be a glass of champagne, a martini or a sherry

White wine (to accompany a light starter)

Followed by red (as the meal gets heavier)

Sweet dessert wine for the dessert

Port with cheese course

A digestif (such as brandy) to go with coffee

Whether you pay any attention to this is up to you, but can I just make a plea for champagne? It's the perfect way to start an evening – even an informal one – and one glass on arrival is always lovely. Champagne is festive, a treat and immediately lifts any occasion. Of course, it doesn't have to be real champagne, either – it can be Cava or anything else fizzy as long as it's reasonably good quality and dry, not sweet.

When inviting friends for dinner, I always ask them to arrive half an hour early for 'cocktails'. This is usually something very simple like a Kir Royale (cassis and champagne) or a champagne cocktail (angostura bitters on a sugar cube, topped with champagne). Although, it doesn't take much to talk me into making raspberry martinis! Offering cocktails before dinner is a great way of getting people there on time, too, as who wants to miss out on a glass of champagne? None of my friends, that's for sure.

WHEN TO SERVE BEER

Beer might seem a less classy option, but sometimes it's the only drink that will do. Also, some people simply prefer drinking beer to wine, and if your guests are beer-lovers make sure to offer it. I wouldn't serve beer at a smart dinner party, but it goes particularly well with less formal affairs. Beer is a perfect partner for barbecues, picnics, and when you have a few friends round for a very informal supper.

And if you're paying for a take-out for everyone, while they watch videos at your place, what's better than an ice-cold beer? It's well-suited to any food that is deep-fried or greasy such as fish 'n' chips, kebabs, pizza, Indian, Thai, Chinese and even Mexican chilli. Of course you can drink wine with these, too, if you want, but often beer just sits better.

TEA AND COFFEE

It's a great shame to spend lots of time, effort (and money) on a wonderful dinner party then at the end of the evening offer your guests a cup of instant coffee to send them on their way. This last drink of the evening is just as important as the welcoming first drink.

As you're probably tired by now and a bit worse for wear, make life easy and get the coffee tray prepared beforehand, with cups, spoons, sugar, milk jug and the coffee measured out in the cafetière ready for the boiling water. Offer decaffeinated too, as well as regular tea and herbal. By this point your guests will probably be pretty full, so don't bother with a big plate of biscuits – a small amaretti, individually-wrapped biscuit with a cup of coffee is a perfect, stylish end to the evening.

YOUR FIVE-MINUTE CHECKLIST

→ Think about your guests and their drinking habits – are they big drinkers? Are any of them teetotal or driving? Plan accordingly.

→ Ask for help. There is plenty of advice on hand when buying wine. Read labels and learn about what *you* like, not what's fashionable.

→ Don't get too hung up about matching wine to food. The rules are fairly straightforward and have relaxed considerably over the years.

→ Make an effort to provide a variety of drinks for non-drinkers. And never pressure anyone to drink alcohol.

> → Make space for chilling drink well before your event, and get your bar ready to alleviate any last-minute panics. You don't want to be playing hunt-the-corkscrew when your guests arrive, or rinsing dirty glasses.

MISTAKES TO AVOID

I'M GOING TO THE TROUBLE OF MAKING DINNER FOR THEM – THEY CAN'T EXPECT FANCY WINE, TOO

Oh yes they can. You don't have to spend a fortune but don't let down your meal with bog-standard drink. Just a little effort goes a long way, and the same applies to non-alcoholic drinks. If buying juice, go for the superior, freshly squeezed variety (rather than the long-life tasteless kind). It will cost you a bit more but it is worth it.

I'M REALLY GOING TO IMPRESS THEM WITH THIS CHÂTEAUNEUF-DU-PAPE, BECAUSE IT COSTS A FORTUNE

Unless your guests are wine buffs, you're wasting your money. Rather than choose something prestigious, think about the flavours of your meal, think about the flavours of your wine, and go for something you genuinely *like*.

I HAVE TO SUPPLY LOTS OF ALCOHOL OTHERWISE IT WILL BE A DISASTER

Not true. You can hold an event with no alcohol if you want – it's up to you. The most important thing to consider is what type of party you're having, the time of day and what your friends' drinking habits are. Supplying lots of alcohol is not a prerequisite for a great party.

8 MUSIC AND ENTERTAINMENT

Think of the best, big party you've been to – one that was held at a hired venue and at which you had a fantastic time. Chances are if you stayed till they started sweeping up around you it was because you were dancing to some great music. Music is an important element of entertaining. It can make or kill any event. There will be some events for which music isn't as important, say if you're holding an event alfresco, a barbecue for instance. But even the humblest of picnics can be livened up with a tape recorder and a few compilation tapes of your friends' favourite artists.

Whatever your event, music works because it helps people relax. Putting some tunes on the stereo before guests arrive is also a great way of relaxing yourself while you do any last-minute preparations, and is probably a better way of alleviating any nerves than downing a few drinks. Also, as your guests appear, there's nothing better than for them to walk into a house that sounds alive with music. It's all part and parcel of making an impact. Stimulate practically all their senses on arrival, with some stylish decor, the aroma of wonderful cooking, a glass of something delicious to drink and, of course, some relaxing music wafting through the house.

WHY MUSIC MATTERS

'Music has a big emotional impact on people,' says William Higham, a marketing and trends consultant who's worked in the music industry for fifteen years, for companies such as Sony, Virgin and Universal. 'We associate certain emotions with music, especially music we've heard before. It may be a relatively new song you were dancing to at a club recently, or a song that reminds you of your teens. It's a relaxer – a bit like that first glass of wine. If you walk into a room of people but there's no music, it can be quite intimidating.'

Music can instantly create a mood, and as such is very useful for your event. For example, if you're holding a dinner party you may want to start your evening with something upbeat, that's familiar to all and puts everyone at ease, such as Dusty Springfield. Once you sit down for dinner, try to choose something equally easy to listen to and upbeat, for example The Cardigans. Your guests will reflect the mood of the music – an upbeat track will create more energy around the dinner table. Then, as the evening develops, slows down and you want people to really chill out, try Massive Attack or Morcheeba. Match your music to the mood you want to create. It sounds obvious, but your choice of music really makes a difference to the way people feel.

Also, think about your guests, their ages, and what their preferences might be. The past decade has seen a trend for rediscovering 'easy listening' (such as Frank Sinatra) and this kind of music is often a fairly safe bet, as it cuts through generations and most people recognise it and like it. 'One of the reasons that chill-out music has sold so well recently,' says William, 'is because more and more of us are having dinner parties and want something that's relaxing and going to be easy to listen to.'

HOW LOUD IS LOUD ENOUGH?

This depends on the kind of party you're holding. If you're inviting people to dance, the music should be pretty loud. People feel inhibited dancing to music if it isn't all-encompassing. Make sure the lighting is subdued and that there are no glaring overhead lights on the dancers, either, or you'll find that nobody takes to the dance floor. Try to create a mood and ambience that is welcoming and feels 'safe' in which to dance – not one where guests feels as if they're on exhibition. (See Chapter 5 to find out how to use lighting well.)

If you're holding a drinks party and want people to chat and mingle, keep the music on reasonably loud but not so loud that guests can't hear each other. You may want to have it on a bit quieter at the beginning and turn it up as the party kicks off and gets livelier throughout the evening. For a dinner party, keep the music very much in the background as the whole point is to have a conversation over a meal. The music should be loud enough to add a backdrop, without intruding or being too noticeable.

There are some parties, of course, where the music is the centre of attention, such as at a kids' party, where you may want to play musical chairs, or get professional entertainers along to get the children singing to well-known songs. Children love singing, and learn from repetition, so music is important when planning a children's party. As the children get older, they'll probably want to be more in charge of the music themselves, so get a portable CD player, ask them to bring along all their favourites and let them take over (see Chapter 16).

WHERE TO PLAY MUSIC

If you're holding your event at home, you're probably limited as to where the music will be played, depending on where your stereo is. Although it's preferable to have the music on in the actual room where you're doing the entertaining, sometimes that's not possible. It's perfectly OK to have the music on in one room (say the living room) and to be eating in the kitchen or dining room. Just make sure you adjust the volume so that you can hear it when seated. Of course the down side of this is that you will have to go backwards and forwards every now and again to add a new tune, but most CDs last the best part of an hour so that shouldn't become too much of a pain. You can even make a virtue of it and get your guests to take it in turns to go and choose something they'd like to hear.

If you have the time and the inclination, you may want to consider bringing your speakers into the dining area, but only do this if you can avoid people tripping on wires by keeping them tucked away out of sight. Failing that, there's nothing wrong with using a portable cassette/CD player if you want it on in the same room. As long as the sound quality is reasonably good, that's OK. Keep it away from the table itself but within handy reach for changing tapes/CDs.

Obviously, if your party is a dancing one you really need the music on in the same room. You also need to be aware when the music's coming to an end so that you can quickly play the next tune. People desert the dance floor as soon as there's a pause. If you don't want to spend all night playing DJ, ask a good friend who loves music to take on this task for you, or share it between a couple of people.

GETTING THE TUNES READY

As with every other element of entertaining, it's vital to get the music prepared beforehand. This won't take long but will save you time and trouble later in the evening when you want to be focusing on your guests. Here are some tips to get you prepared:

→ At least a week before the event, think about what kind of party it is and whether you need to pay particular attention to the music. Is it a themed party? (A 20s cocktail party is crying out for 20s music.) Are there guests coming who won't like the same kind of music as you (for example, a teen's birthday party where the latest chart hits are a must)? Is it a daytime event with a real mix of ages and types of people, such as a tea party? In this case you may want to go for something a bit safe like classic tunes, big band music or easy listening.

→ Consider whether you need to buy/borrow your music or whether you have what you need. William recommends trying your local library, 'Or visit one of the large record stores; they often have big world music sections. If you're having, say a Moroccan evening, try going for the compilation CDs you can now get; strictly speaking, they may not be that authentic, but you don't want to get too anal about the whole thing. Also, you don't want something that intrudes so much that it puts everyone on edge and becomes the focal point.'

→ Think about how long your event is going on for and how much music you need. There's nothing wrong with playing the same tracks more than once, but a lot of repetition can be annoying and looks like you only have one CD or album! For a dinner party that lasts from 7.30 till, say, midnight, I'd recommend having about six CDs or albums to hand.

→ On the day of the party, get your music out and put it next to the stereo so you're all set to go. 'If you're having a house party with guests that you don't know well,' says William, 'assign someone to keep an eye on the CD player. This will stop somebody hijacking it for the duration of the evening and putting on just everything they want to hear.'

→ An hour before guests arrive, put on one of your favourite albums or CDs to relax you and get you into the party spirit.

→ Make sure that music is playing when your first guests arrive. This is particularly important if you are holding a big party, as *someone* has to arrive first and music can stop them from feeling embarrassed or uncomfortable. It also fills any awkward silences during the initial conversation.

WHAT TO PLAY

Only you know what you like and what your guests are likely to appreciate. Remember that this isn't a time to pander to your eclectic musical tastes. The object is to play music that everyone can enjoy, and perhaps that means going for something a little more mainstream than you'd normally choose.

DON'T BE PRECIOUS

Unless you're entertaining a posse of DJs (in which case, frankly, they should bring along their own music) there's no need to get too hung up on the music you choose. Your guests don't have to *adore* your music, as long as they don't hate it, either. Choose what you like, but avoid anything with offensive or aggressive lyrics. This is not the time to bring out your Eminem collection. Hardcore rap may be great for a dancing party, but not the best choice if you've got the in-laws round for dinner.

And, however passionate you may be about music, try not to be *too* boring about. Men, in particular, are prone to being very trainspottery when it comes to their music collection and there's nothing duller than listening to someone droning on about why *this* version of a particular song is better than the one they're about to play you. The music during a dinner party is for background enjoyment. Discussing it at length alienates any guests who don't have the same knowledge as you or, frankly, are just not that interested.

FANCY YOURSELF AS A DJ?

Making compilation tapes for a party can be great fun, especially if you're having a themed party and already have an extensive collection of music. 'You can make a tape for your party, or burn a CD with all the various types of music you'll want to play throughout the evening,' says William. 'With high-tech compilations, they can last for hours. I'd recommend making a few tapes, then you have more flexibility and you can change them as and when you want to change the mood rather than having to wait to get to the bit you want. People might not feel like dancing till later, so putting dancing music on before the party is really ready for it can ruin the atmosphere. You want the transition to be seamless, as if you were a DJ.'

Ideas for themed music

Moroccan evening: belly dancing music

Hallowe'en party: Sisters of Mercy, Marilyn Manson, anything goth

School disco night: dig out those 80s classics (preferably on vinyl!)

Bad taste party: Eurodisco

Compilations are also great ways of getting all your favourite tracks together and work particularly well for dancing parties. Many record companies now sell ready-made themed compilation CDs and tapes, so you can choose every mood from 'chill out' to 'Ibiza summer'.

Of course you may want to make your own compilation tapes. If you do, make sure you allow yourself plenty of time because this is a very time-consuming venture. Start compiling your tapes as soon as you know you're having a party. It really is a labour of love and you may find you spend days doing just one tape, especially if you decide to theme them. The great thing, of course, is that once compiled you can use these tapes time and again. Playing DJ in this way can also add to the feeling of excitement and anticipation around an event, and helps you look forward to it. Try not to take your efforts too seriously, though, and always have some CD back-ups in case your tapes don't go down well with people who want to dance. After all, there's no accounting for taste.

CALLING IN THE PROFESSIONALS

There are times when it's best to leave the music to the professionals. If you're planning a big, important event, such as a wedding reception, you don't want to be faffing around with CDs and tapes. By hiring a professional you are paying someone to take care of the details for you, as well as shoulder the responsibility. And, assuming you find the right person, it really is money well spent. 'If you're hiring a band, try a "tribute" band,' says William. 'These are bands that do cover versions. You can find them on the

Internet and there seems to be a real trend for them at the moment.'

If you're hiring a venue you will almost certainly need to pay someone else to provide the music, as you won't be allowed to provide your own. Most venues can recommend someone. (Also see Chapter 11 to discover the best way of hiring professionals for every aspect of your event.)

A FOOLPROOF GUIDE TO HIRING PROFESSIONALS

→ What kind of service do you need? You can hire a DJ, a band, musicians – the choice is endless.

→ Once you've decided, choose a handful of possibles and find out what other events they've performed at. Explain exactly what you want and ask to speak to people they've worked for in the past. Go on personal recommendation whenever possible.

→ Always go and see a live band or performer before booking or ask for a tape or video.

→ Consider having more than one type of music. A friend of mine had a string quartet in her house for a birthday party. They played downstairs (no amplification needed, hence no electricity problems), then in another part of the house she had contemporary music on for anyone who wanted to dance. Big nightclubs often have various areas for different 'music moods'. If your venue is big enough it *is* possible to divide up the music areas in this way. For my wedding reception, I had a pianist playing Cole Porter in the dining area, where most of the older family guests stayed for the evening, and at the same time a disco downstairs for our friends. A perfect solution for dealing with the fact that it was a very mixed crowd.

→ Consider your venue and what the DJ/band's requirements will be. If your party is at home, you need to check that your electricity supply will be adequate for their needs. You won't make yourself very popular with the neighbours if you blow the lights for the whole street. If your DJ/band are working in a venue, ask them to check requirements directly with the venue's representative.

→ Be clear and specific about what your needs are. Tell them exactly the sort of music you want (and make sure they have it, in the case of a DJ, or can play it in the case of a band). There's no point asking a ragtime band to do a Beatles set, so do make sure you're choosing the right person for the job in hand. Music is more important to some people than others. If you're passionate about it, don't be embarrassed to list your requirements. At our wedding reception, my partner Andrew prepared the DJ by giving him a list of songs to play, and even provided the music when he didn't have specific tracks. The result was that we had exactly the disco we wanted and our friends enjoyed a great night dancing.

→ If the DJ/ band are unfamiliar with the venue ask them to visit it before the day. That way they'll see the space they'll be working in and can discuss any possible problems ahead of time with the venue manager on site.

→ Check what time they will start, how long they will play for, whether there will be a break and if they need a sound check (get them to do this before guests arrive). If the band or DJ are going to have a break during the evening, what music will be provided until they return?

→ Ask what your DJ/ band will be wearing if it matters to you.

→ A DJ may need a longer time to set up as they have to organise their sound system and often lighting too. Make sure you take this into account.

→ Sign a contract!

KARAOKE

The ultimate in DIY musical entertainment has to be the Japanese craze of karaoke. Here, you sing along to your favourite tunes with the help of a microphone and lyrics on a TV screen. There are several karaoke machines for sale on the market or you can hire them, and they've been a popular addition to many a party.

Karaoke should be seen as a bit of spontaneous fun rather than a competitive sport. If you want karaoke at your event, remember that not everyone may be up for it. Don't force people into singing if they really are not that way inclined, and only organise karaoke for the *whole* evening if you know that your guests will love it. (How to find out? Ask them!)

Karaoke can be particularly popular with children, but make sure that the songs provided include their favourites. Once they get to the age of around eight, children become very discerning with their musical taste and what they loved a month ago they may consider very uncool now. Remember, irony is lost on children, so even though you may think the songs from *Grease* are a great way to pass the time, they won't.

GAMES AND OTHER ENTERTAINMENT

'Kids' themes work well for adults,' says Danielle Nay, MD of Dr Party, a company that specialises in themed parties, 'and generally, people like games, like Twister, Operation, and Ker-plunk. They're the games we grew up with. You can hire giant versions of all these games for parties. (See Resources chapter.) Dig out the games during a party if you want, but make it inclusive and don't bully anyone into playing something they really don't want to.

Of course, if your guests are willing there's no need to stop there. Adults can play anything kids can – Twister, pass the parcel, musical chairs. For the slightly more sophisticated taste, try one of the many Murder Mystery dinner party games on offer. These come in boxes, complete with 'character cards' and clues. Tell guests what you're planning and only invite those who want to take part.

The idea is that guests arrive in character (possibly in fancy dress) and the mystery unfolds as they play throughout the evening. It's interspersed with various courses. Great fun for extroverts, especially with people you don't know very well. (For ideas on games to play with children, see Chapter 16, which looks at children's parties in more detail.)

YOUR FIVE-MINUTE CHECKLIST

→ Use music to welcome your guests. It'll create an atmosphere even in an empty room.
→ Think about the mood you want to create, the occasion and the guests invited. Choose accordingly.
→ Plan ahead so you're not scrabbling around at the last minute.
→ If using professionals, be sure they have performed at this kind of event before, are qualified to do so and know exactly what's required. Don't be embarrassed about spelling it out, in writing preferably.

MISTAKES TO AVOID

WE DON'T NEED MUSIC – WE'LL TALK TO EACH OTHER

Even the most gregarious guests will appreciate some music in the background. And there will come a point in the evening when the conversation dries up, even if it is for a minute. Music smooths over awkward silences, creates a relaxed atmosphere and generally pulls the event together. Don't skimp on it.

I'LL JUST PLAY ALL MY FAVOURITE STUFF

Who are you entertaining, yourself or others? Think about what your guests may like to hear. If they hate your taste in music, ask them to contribute a CD each that they'd like others to hear. That way you'll keep everyone happy. Better still, if you're theming a party then theme the music too. I sat in a fantastic, beautiful Chinese restaurant once that played tinny Euro disco all night. The wrong music can ruin the ambience you've striven to create.

YOU'VE GOT TO HEAR THIS REMIX FROM THE 1982 ALBUM...

No really, don't bother. I promise you that nobody is going to be as fascinated as you are. They may feign interest because, after all, you're the host. Don't be a music bore or take it too seriously.

WHAT DO YOU MEAN YOU DON'T WANT TO PLAY STRIP POKER?

If you're playing games, don't bully people into taking part. Respect the fact that some people simply aren't as outgoing as others. And never leave one person who doesn't want to join in sitting in the corner feeling ostracised. If it's a small group, either all of you should play or none of you.

9 THE AFTERMATH

A party isn't over until your house or venue is back in order. And until then, you're in a sort of Party Twilight Zone. Nobody enjoys clearing up after an event as it can be time-consuming and messy. But unless you're feeling flush, chances are the job will fall on your shoulders. This chapter looks at how to make the process a whole lot easier, faster and, yes, even perhaps rather enjoyable. But, of course, you can't start until all your guests have left.

THE GUEST WHO WOULDN'T GO

Some guests seem oblivious to the fact that a party is over, either because they've had too much to drink or are simply a bit thick-skinned. Short of putting on your pyjamas, bidding them goodnight and climbing the stairs, it can be difficult to get the message across without being curt. But there *are* some tactics you can use that are guaranteed to get results without causing offence.

SET A TIME LIMIT

It may sound like great fun to let your party continue until the early hours, but this is only the case if you have the energy to keep going, too. As host you have to stay coherent, entertaining and upright throughout the whole event. You may also want to set time limits out of consideration to others; perhaps you have children sleeping upstairs, or an elderly neighbour that you don't want to keep up all night.

It's perfectly acceptable to indicate a time limit for your event when sending out the invitations. You may be inviting guests to a daytime event, such as a tea party, barbecue or an 'at home' where they can pop in between certain times (say, 2 p.m.–5 p.m.). If you're inviting them for dinner, send out invitations that specify 'drinks at 7 p.m., dinner from 8–11'. On very formal invitations you may still find phrases like 'carriages at 1 a.m.', which is a discreet way of saying that the event ends at 1 a.m. Far from being rude, guests will understand the message and often like to know what to expect from the evening.

If your event is less formal, and you're inviting friends verbally, you can get round the issue by saying that dinner is at, say, eight o'clock and you envisage the evening ending around midnight. Keep in mind that if you have a party and don't specify a time limit, guests may well assume that it isn't an issue for you.

If your event is held in a hired venue, you'll have agreed the time limits on signing the contract so be sure to understand them. Does your agreement include enough time to get into the venue and make any preparations needed (e.g. decorations, setting up a disco)? Will you be expected to have cleared up at the end of the evening, or can you have extra time to do this the next day? Better still, can you pay for someone else to do it instead? If you overstay your welcome in a hired venue you may well be charged extra – ask about this at the time of booking, as on the day you may want your event to continue. (Also make sure any extension incorporates the bar licence too!) For more information on booking venues, see Chapter 11.

CALL THEM A TAXI

If a couple of your guests show no signs of leaving (despite the fact that everyone else has said their goodbyes) chances are they've had a few too many drinks. Most of us pick up on signals that the night is over, but once we've had a few drinks that sensitivity and intuition goes out of the window. Ask if you can call them a cab, or if they are really worse for wear just order one and then tell them 'Your cab's here!' They probably won't even remember that they didn't order one.

If you know the time your event will end, because it's at a venue, pre-book a few cabs from various cab companies so guests don't have to wait too long. As the evening draws to a close, let them know that you have some taxis arriving in a few minutes if they want to go and claim one. It's a thoughtful gesture and will be appreciated, as there's nothing worse than waiting ages for a lift home.

STOP TIPSY GUESTS DRIVING HOME

Ask someone else who's sober to give them a lift or let them stay
the night. They can come back for their car the next day, or you
may want to try one of the new drive-your-car services around. A
driver turns up on a folding bike that they then put into the boot of
the guest's car and drive them home. For details see the Resources
section of this book.

SERVE SOME COFFEE

Preparing some coffee (or tea) at the end of a dinner party is a
good way of letting guests know that the evening is coming to an
end. Don't expect people to leave immediately afterwards, as they
may want to chat for a while.

TELL THEM HOW MUCH FUN IT'S BEEN

Ask guests if they've had a good time, thank them for coming and
talk about the party in the past tense ('It's been great seeing you
after all this time. We must do it again soon.'). This is a subtle way
of saying that the party is over and most people will realise it's time
to go. If they won't get the hint and seem intent on staying, ask
them how they're planning to get home and if you can call a cab for
them. Remember to do it with charm and try not to look fed up or
tired.

CHANGE THE ATMOSPHERE

If they really won't leave, then you're going to have to be a bit more
obvious. Changing the atmosphere of the room should do the trick.
The easiest way to do this is to increase the lighting (just gently
turn up a dimmer rather than putting on overhead lights, which will
seem rude) and turn down the music. You can even try opening a
window or start clearing up a little bit. Clearing up while your
guests are still present is usually considered a no-no, but frankly if
someone simply won't go I think there's nothing wrong with it. As
long as you don't start clattering plates in the kitchen and
slamming doors.

FOR THE *REALLY* THICK-SKINNED

Every now and again you'll come across a guest who's decided that they'd like to stay. For good. If they're not taking the hints, you're going to have to be blatant about asking them to leave. Try something like, 'I'm glad you've had such a good time, but I'm afraid we really have to call it a night.' Still no response? Try, 'Let me get your coat for you'. If they're really that insensitive to your needs, help them on with their coat and show them the door. Don't be embarrassed. They probably won't remember it the next day.

CLEARING UP

Throwing a party always seems like such a hospitable, fun idea until the morning after when you're faced with dirty glasses, full ashtrays and a blocked sink. I don't know anyone who actually enjoys the clearing up process, but there *are* ways of making it easier and more bearable.

Of course good sense would tell you to clear up before you go to bed, but few of us have the energy to do that. What you decide to do really depends on how tired you are, what time it is and what you're facing. If you *can* clear up before going to bed, good on you. I tend to do this after dinner parties, as I don't like the idea of waking up to it. But if I've had a bigger party, I leave it to the next day.

HOW TO MAKE CLEANING UP EASIER

Get some help: if you share a house, make it clear (before you throw the party) that you'd like some help in clearing up. If you have friends staying over who offer to help, accept. Don't be a martyr – you'll get it done a lot faster if there are two or three of you.

Put some music on: you may as well *try* to have a good time whilst doing this.

Pile up the really nasty dishes: these are the cooking pots and serving plates. Put them to one side and pour hot water and detergent on them, letting them soak.

Soak crockery and cutlery in a bowl: keep it there for a few minutes while you zoom round the rest of the house.

Get out the bin liners: throw away any leftovers that haven't been refrigerated and empty ashtrays. If it was an informal party, expect to find paper plates everywhere. Don't forget to look in all the rooms that may have been used by guests, including the bathroom. If it's summer, check the garden for any debris.

Collect bottles and cans for recycling: as well as being environmentally friendly, this limits the amount of debris you have to shove into black bin liners.

Throw open some windows: and get the stale smell of wine/beer and food out of the house. Especially important if you had guests who smoked. (Of course, you remembered to shut any bedroom doors to stop the smoke getting in, right?)

Return to the washing: tackle the crockery and cutlery first, then the glasses last. Wash the serving dishes only when they've had a good soaking.

Finishing touches: plump up cushions and vacuum or sweep up. Done.

CLEARING UP AT A VENUE

If you're hiring a venue, you may not have the option of leaving the clearing up to the next day. Your contract may state that you must get the venue in good order before you leave for the evening. Find out before you book, and if possible get a friend or family member to help you do this. If it's your wedding reception, for heaven's sake get someone else to take this on! Ask if the venue can provide a cleaner (it will cost, of course), or hire one yourself for a couple of hours. It really is worth paying someone else to do this if you can. Don't forget you may also have to:

→ Take down decorations
→ Return any equipment you've hired or borrowed (glasses, crockery, chairs)
→ Get the DJ/ band to dismantle and remove their equipment

Popular venues often have back-to-back bookings, hence the need for you to clear up and get out as soon as possible after the event ends. Plan ahead and rope in a team of friends beforehand, so they know their help is needed at the end of the evening.

THANKING PEOPLE

Just as it's important to welcome your guests at the door, and make sure they know you're pleased to see them, try if possible to always say goodbye and thank them for coming. During very big parties guests sometimes slip away, so you may not always know who's still there or who has left.

If you've received any gifts during the party (perhaps it was your birthday, a housewarming or your wedding reception) do make sure you find the time to write a thank you note. It's a shame that this seems to be a bit of a dying social tradition. If a thank you note feels too formal give them a call or send an email instead. And if you hired a professional who went above and beyond the call of duty (say a fantastic caterer or DJ), send them a thank you note, saying you will recommend them to others, too. It's useful to build up a good relationship with these people as you may want to use them again.

GOODY BAGS

Some people give goody bags to departing guests, as a little thank you and a way of making the event last just that bit longer. At the Oscars, the guests are given bags with extravagant pressies like Gucci sunglasses and Tiffany jewellery. Back in the real world, you may want to give guests a little reminder of your party. Maria Hipwell and Liz Ellerton are founders of bespoke gift company, Lilies and Chips. They say, 'Goody bags are popular in celebrity circles, and they're a great way to get people talking about your party days after the event. They don't have to be expensive – you can give people a hangover kit, for example, if you're having a cocktail party. It's a thank you, and a way of saying "remember this party as one of the best you've been to".'

This can work particularly well for themed parties, where you can continue the theme into the goody bag. So, for example, at a Hallowe'en party you can give your guests a bag of 'trick or treat' sweets; at a colour-themed party, colour theme all the pressies in the bag, too. Children love goody bags and they're practically *de rigueur* now. See Chapter 16 for more ideas on children's goody bags.

DEALING WITH THE NEIGHBOURS

If you're having a dinner party for four, there's no reason to worry about the neighbours (unless you have very raucous friends), but when you invite larger numbers invariably it affects those around you. Hopefully you'll have warned your neighbours about your party before the day itself. This gives them a chance to accept the fact that it could get noisy. It also enables them to make other plans if they don't want to be home when the party takes place. If you get on well with your neighbours, invite them along, too. Even if they don't accept, it's unlikely that they will then complain about the noise.

Elderly people in particular, or those with young families, will find noise more of a disturbance than others. It's a nice gesture to give neighbours a bottle of wine left over from the party or perhaps a bunch of flowers, to say thank you for their tolerance.

SO, WAS IT A GOOD PARTY?

After every event, big or small, formal or informal, it's a good idea to take stock. Did it go according to plan? Was it the party you wanted it to be? What could have gone better? What would you do differently next time? As with everything, practice makes perfect. The more entertaining you do, the more confidence you'll gain and the better you'll get at it. If you enjoy entertaining and seem to invite the same group of friends round for dinner quite a lot, it's worth making a note of what you cooked, so that you don't make the same dish too often.

HOW TO DEAL WITH HANGOVERS

Unless you're teetotal you will have, at some point, suffered the hangover from hell. But as a host you really shouldn't drink too much as you won't be able to attend to your guests' needs. So here are some tips to help prevent a hangover – or if the worst happens, help alleviate it.

→ Before the party, drink a glass of milk or eat a cheese sandwich. If you have fat in your stomach the alcohol will metabolise much slower.
→ Intersperse your alcoholic drinks with plenty of water or soft drinks.

→ Drink as much water as you can before going to bed. If you manage to ward off dehydration you won't get that thumping headache.

→ The next day, if you're feeling rough, try ibuprofen with some food. Aspirin may upset your stomach and paracetamol isn't kind to the liver (which has already taken a battering).

→ Toast with jam should help get your blood sugars back on form.

→ A greasy breakfast may be in order if you can stomach it, but it will probably leave you sleepy.

→ Don't drink any more. The 'hair of the dog' is a myth.

→ Don't do a workout. It's the worst thing you can do with a hangover as you're already dehydrated. But *do* take some gentle exercise (e.g. a walk outdoors) to start your metabolism working on that alcohol.

YOUR FIVE-MINUTE CHECKLIST

→ Some guests need a nudge to leave. Don't be embarrassed about calling cabs for people or using whatever tactics it takes to make it clear that the evening is almost over. As long as it's done with charm, nobody will take offence.

→ Before hiring a venue, check what their rules are about clearing up and when you'd be expected to do it.

→ Get some help and have a system for clearing up. Put each person in charge of a separate task.

→ Don't forget to thank guests for coming and for any gifts you may have received.

MISTAKES TO AVOID

FOR GOD'S SAKE, JUST GET OUT WILL YOU?

There are better ways of asking guests to leave. You can be assertive without being rude. If someone proves difficult, smile, put on the charm and just vow never to invite them again.

MAKE MINE A DOUBLE

A drunk host is a big no-no. Yes, have a good time but pace yourself. If you get out of control so will your party. Remember, you're the one steering this ship!

10 STAYING OVER

Inviting a guest to spend the night at your house after an event is the ultimate in hospitality. You may have fond memories of your student days when everyone just fell into a corner at the end of a party. When you're eighteen, sleeping for a couple of hours in a cramped corner using your coat as a blanket is no big deal because sleep just isn't a priority at that age. But as we get older the demands on us increase and our needs change. From the age of about mid-twenties onwards, most of us recoil at the thought of spending a night lying in a sleeping bag on a crisp-strewn carpet.

With age, we crave the comfort of our own bed and familiar surroundings. That said, there are times when sleeping over is simply unavoidable, so the good host's job is to find ways of making the experience as comfortable as possible. It's not just a case of pointing out the bed. There *is* an art to making friends feel welcome in your home, and the secret lies in considering their every possible need.

When you invite people to your event, think about if they may need to stay over and – if you have the space – do offer a bed for the night. This can make the difference between someone accepting your invitation or declining. If you don't have a spare bed, but can offer something less comfy instead – such as the sofa or a sleeping bag for example – still extend the invitation to stay but make it clear that that's where they'll be sleeping. If you do a lot of entertaining and don't have a spare bedroom, it's worth investing in a sofa-bed or a futon that folds up into a sofa when not in use.

WHY GUESTS MAY NEED TO STAY OVER

There are several reasons a guest may need to stay overnight, but here are the most common ones:

→ They live several miles away and don't want to bother with a return journey the same day.
→ They're visiting you for the weekend.

→ They may want to drink and can't drive back. Or they may have had more to drink than they'd expected to and realise that driving home would be foolish.

→ They don't drive and public transport is unreliable late at night.

→ They can't afford/don't want to pay for a taxi home.

→ It's simply more convenient to return the next day.

WHEN STAYING OVER MAKES SENSE

New Year's Eve: it's bound to be a late-night event and transport won't be reliable.

Cocktail/drinks party: guests don't usually want to go teetotal when everyone else is trying out great cocktails. If they can stay, they can have a few drinks without worrying about getting home.

Girls' night in/pyjama party: many twenty-something women love having their girl friends round for a night of videos, food, chat and a sleepover. It's a bonding thing.

Children's sleepover: once they get to the age of around eight, children really love sleepovers at friends' houses. In recent years these have gained in popularity and have rapidly become part of our culture.

THE IMPROMPTU SLEEPOVER

A good host stays flexible. Most of us, at some point, have offered a guest a bed for the night on the spur of the moment. Or perhaps a guest has asked us at the last minute if they could possibly stay over. If you find yourself in this situation, don't panic. As it's *not* a planned sleepover, expectations will be much lower. Here's the minimum you need to do:

→ Explain where they'll be sleeping if it's not an actual bed, so there are no nasty surprises. If you don't have a spare bed you can improvise with sofa cushions laid on the floor, a sleeping bag or a duvet on the floor. Everyone understands that the convenience factor here will outweigh the comfort one. It probably won't be the best sleep they've ever had, but that doesn't matter. If your guests are either elderly or pregnant, giving up your own bed is the decent thing to do. Otherwise, you're not really expected to, unless you're feeling particularly chivalrous.

→ Provide a warm enough covering and a cushion or pillow to sleep on. We're assuming here that your sheets/duvet and pillowcases are fairly clean, as even an impromptu guest deserves basic standards of hygiene!

→ Before retiring, show them where the shower is and tell them to help themselves to toiletries. Provide a clean towel. They'll have to make do without a toothbrush (unless you happen to have some new ones lying around).

→ Make sure the room is warm enough but also has enough ventilation (show them how to unlock windows if necessary).

THE PLANNED SLEEPOVER

This is a different ball game. If you know beforehand that a guest will be staying over after the event, then there's no excuse really for not making their stay as comfortable as possible. Obviously, the lengths you go to will depend on your space and circumstances and how well you know your guests. If they're family members or very close, chances are they'll have stayed before and will know their way round your kitchen. They won't feel shy about getting up in the morning and making themselves a cup of tea. But if your guests haven't stayed before, do make the effort and treat them like a special guest.

Think of this as an extension to the previous evening. Presumably, you'll have put a lot of work into the night before so why let yourself down by skimping on the details? Making someone feel extra-special can only reflect well on you and, hopefully, will elicit a return invitation!

THE BASICS

Do this the morning of your event or even a couple of days before, to give you a head start.

→ Change the sheets, duvet cover and pillowcases on the guest bed. If guests are sleeping on a sofa bed, vacuum the sofa in advance to make sure you don't find loose change and crumbs down it when you open it for them. If they're using sleeping bags, make sure everything they'll need is to hand (including pillows) so that you don't have to visit the loft at 2 a.m.

→ Provide clean towels (nice ones, please, not scratchy old ones). A large bath towel and a small hand towel per person.

→ Tidy the room or area they'll be sleeping in. If your house is big enough to have a guest bedroom, chances are it's used as a bit of a dumping ground. Remove any items that are in the way, or try to limit them to one corner of the room. Keep obstructions away from the bed itself. Nobody wants to trip over a pile of old magazines at 3 a.m.

→ Ensure privacy. If the room doesn't have curtains or a blind, try draping a throw over a rail. A room with no curtains doesn't allow for much sleep or warmth.

→ If the room has a slightly unlived in feel, install a couple of items from other parts of the house, such as a vase of flowers or a small plant. Try to make it feel homely.

→ Anything personal hanging around? Move it elsewhere.

→ As with an impromptu sleepover, make sure the room is warm enough but also has enough ventilation.

THE EXTRAS

These are the little touches that will be remembered. They really are 'extra' so it's up to you if you want to do them. If your event the previous evening was formal, they're a good idea.

→ Toiletry welcome pack: place a new washcloth, a boxed guest soap, a travel-size shampoo and a new travel toothbrush in a small pile on the guest's bed, on top of their folded towels and invite them to use the supplies. Let them know where the hairdryer is.

→ Place a box of tissues in the room.

→ Put a bedside lamp near the bed.

→ Have a few magazines or paperback books lying around for them to read.

→ Put a small plant or vase of (unscented) flowers in the room. Nothing with lots of pollen (no lilies!).

→ Make sure there's a mirror in the room, either on the wall or a hand-held one, as well as a clean hairbrush and comb.

→ Have a bottle of mineral water or a small carafe of water to hand, and a glass, by the bed.

DON'T FORGET ...

→ To make sure there's enough hot water for everyone to have a shower.

→ If you have a burglar alarm, don't activate it before going to bed as an unsuspecting guest may set it off.

→ If you have any pets, check if your guests have allergies to them. It's quite common to be allergic to cat or dog hair, and this can cause a tightening chest and shortness of breath. If your guests *are* allergic, warn them that they'll need to take their antihistamine beforehand. They may decide not to stay over at all as allergies can make people very uncomfortable.

CHILDREN TO STAY

If you have children, they may at times want to invite their friends to come and stay. Or you may want to invite friends to dinner and are willing to let them bring their children with them, and for all of them to stay over.

One of the best evenings I ever had was New Year's Eve 1999, when instead of going to a big party we decided to have a small dinner party with some friends. They happen to have two small children and, as finding a babysitter on Millennium New Year's Eve was not even worth thinking about, we invited them to bring their children and sleepover at our house. On arrival they put them to bed in our guest room and we got on with celebrating.

WHAT TO CONSIDER WHEN CHILDREN SLEEP OVER

→ Where will they sleep? If they are very young they will need a carry cot. Their parents probably have one they can bring along. Older children love the excitement of sleeping in sleeping bags or sharing a double bed with a friend.

→ Do they need a night light? Many children like a light on all night or at least until they fall asleep. Ask their parents.

→ If you have stairs, make sure toddlers can't fall down them if sleeping upstairs, by either shutting their door or having a gate at the top.

→ Make the house child-friendly. Keep any medications or toxic substances well out of reach. Tidy away any flexes that children may trip over and be especially aware of the area surrounding their bed. Is there anything here that could prove a potential hazard? If you're not very child-minded, ask their parents to give the room a quick look over to make sure you haven't missed anything.

→ Do you need to get any special food or drink in? If they need milk in the morning, find out what kind they drink (children can't drink long-life milk).

→ Do they have any allergies, life-threatening or otherwise, that you should know about? Some children are intolerant to cows' milk, while others may have an allergy to nuts. If you're cooking for children, ask their parents beforehand if there's anything they'd rather you didn't give them. (For more information on children's parties, see Chapter 16.)

THE NEXT DAY

If when you wake knowing that you have guests in the house, you feel like crawling back under the duvet, don't. Unfortunately, a long lie-in when you have house guests isn't really an option. Unless, of course, it's by mutual agreement and you have no plans for the rest of the morning.

If you'd like a lie-in and think they would, too, tell them. Something along the lines of, 'We don't usually get up till around 11 on Sundays, so don't feel you have to rise early' should do the trick. Some guests like to get up and go home, in which case they may leave without you seeing them. Though most will want to stay for breakfast and to say thank you.

WHAT? I HAVE TO MAKE BREAKFAST, TOO?

Yep, you do. It can be as simple or luxurious as you want but the fact is it's rude to wave them off without the offer of a cup of coffee and a piece of toast. These are the very basics you should have to hand: milk, bread, butter, cereal, coffee, tea, juice. Of course, if they're staying for a leisurely breakfast or brunch, it's worth getting some croissants in, maybe making some scrambled eggs, and buying the Sunday papers, too.

Your guests will take your lead. If you're relaxed and look content to sit and read the papers while having another cup of coffee, they will too. If you rush around clattering plates and tidying up, they'll probably feel they should go. And if they look like they may want to stay for lunch, too, a polite way of getting them to leave is by asking what they have planned for the rest of the day. That gives you a chance to mention any plans you may have and tell them if you need to be at a particular place by a certain time.

PLACE STILL A MESS?

If you still haven't cleared up from the night before, you may get some offers of help. Don't be shy in taking them up on it. It's a good way of them showing their gratitude for your hospitality, and will be a lot quicker than having to do it all yourself. (For other tips on clearing up after a party, see Chapter 9.) You may not want to bother with preparing breakfast if your kitchen is a mess, so why not suggest going to a local café instead?

YOUR FIVE-MINUTE CHECKLIST

→ Always explain where somebody will be sleeping if it's not in a bed.
→ Unless they're an impromptu guest, prepare their sleeping area well in advance.
→ Add little touches to make someone's stay extra-special. Do this by anticipating what they may need and thinking about what *you'd* appreciate in their situation.
→ You're still playing host, so keep up the charm and never make guests feel like you've had enough and just wish they'd leave, however tired you are.
→ Be extra careful when your house guests are children. Make the house child-friendly and find out about food preferences.

MISTAKES TO AVOID

WHY DON'T YOU ALL STAY OVER? WE'VE PLENTY OF ROOM!

Think carefully. Do you have enough bed or floor space for fifteen people? What are they going to use as blankets? Pillows? How will you cope in the morning? It may seem like a wonderful gesture at the time, but you'll be tired tomorrow and you'll be kicking yourself as you make fifteen rounds of toast.

THE CAB COMPANY SAYS THEY CAN GET YOU HOME FOR £52, WHICH SOUNDS QUITE REASONABLE TO ME. OR IF YOU CUT THROUGH THE WOODS YOU CAN GET THE NIGHT BUS.

Don't expect people to do ridiculous things to go home. If it's expensive or if their personal safety is at risk, do invite them to stay. They will be so grateful that they probably won't mind if it means sleeping on the floor. In future, think about this beforehand and plan ahead!

ANYWAY, I'M OFF TO BED NOW. DON'T BOTHER WAKING ME BEFORE YOU GO.

Aaagh! There are subtler ways of letting them know you're tired. Never go to bed before the last guest has, and if you'd like a lie-in the next day, tell them what time you usually get up. They'll either do the same or will let themselves out. Making them feel unwelcome is unforgivable.

11 HIRING PROFESSIONALS

However capable, multi-skilled and wonderfully talented you are, the fact remains that there will come a time when you need to call in the experts. The trick is knowing when that is. This chapter looks at identifying when you need help, how to hire professionals, what to ask them and how to make sure you get exactly the service you want.

HOW TO KNOW WHEN YOU NEED HELP

There is nothing wrong with asking for help. In fact, if you open practically any business manual or 'how-I-made-it-big' biography, you'll find that successful people always draw on the expert resources of those around them. Delegation is what it's all about, and this applies to entertaining as much as it does to the world of work. Consider the following when deciding if you need to pay for professional help.

1. IMPORTANCE OF THE OCCASION

If you're planning something momentous – a wedding, big anniversary, important work function or any formal event – it's worth getting as much professional help as possible. These are the kind of once-in-a-lifetime events that you can't afford to allow to go wrong (unlike a dinner party, say, where if the food isn't quite as good as you'd hoped you can always get away with it if you have a bit of charm, and maybe invite them again once your kitchen skills have improved). Professional help can be anything from a caterer to waiting staff to a florist or hired band, depending on the nature of your event.

2. THE FORMALITY OF THE OCCASION

A general rule of thumb is that the more formal your event, the more hired help you will need. This is not just because of size (most formal events tend to be large ones) but also because you need to make sure that everything about the occasion is 'polished' and the whole thing runs smoothly.

3. NUMBER OF GUESTS INVITED

Any event with over twenty people can be exhausting for the host – whether it's a picnic or a dinner. It's obvious really, but the more people you invite, the more work you'll have to do. And don't believe anyone that tells you that cooking for thirty is really no different to cooking for six. It's a lie. (How are you going to fit all that food in your oven, for a start? And do you have enough plates, cutlery and glasses?)

If you really don't want to hire any help, keep your event small. If you insist on inviting large numbers but don't want to get help in, you'll have to delegate certain duties to friends (like playing barperson all night, or taking coats).

4. YOUR BUDGET

Oh yes, money! Don't consider hiring anyone until you've worked out a budget. It won't take long, will save you hassle and can help you focus on where your priorities lie. For example, it may be that you want to throw a dancing party and your priority is the music, so spend your money on a good DJ rather than on the catering. Or perhaps you want to splash out on the decor for a swish Christmas drinks party, and you need the help of a local florist to 'dress' the room.

Think through the type of event you're having, the atmosphere you want to create and then look at the money you want to spend on it. See Chapter 3 for easy ways to decide on a budget.

5. YOUR TIME

The less you have, the more you may need to call in the experts. They can help save time by doing the work for you, that's why enlisting their help can feel a bit decadent. Try not to feel guilty about this as it means you can focus on other aspects of your event. Do note, though, that anyone who is very good will be booked up for several weeks so a certain amount of planning is still called for. Don't fall into the trap of hiring just anyone because you're desperate. If your invitations haven't gone out yet, it's preferable to postpone the date of your event until you can get the experts you want. You're going to be paying for a service, so why compromise? For more information on budgeting your time (as well as your money) see Chapter 3.

6. YOUR ABILITIES!

Want to create all the hot canapés for that spontaneous event you've just invited fifty people to? Great. Good on you. We assume you'll be booking into a sanatorium the day after? Unless you've got fantastic culinary skills, more than one oven, experience in catering for numbers, and lots of time on your hands, don't even think about it. Instead, hire someone who has successfully catered for dozens of events like yours, knows all the possible pitfalls and is guaranteed to make sure it goes smoothly. Be honest about your abilities and don't skimp on hiring a professional if it's blatantly clear that you need one.

WHO'S FOR HIRE?

Today, you can hire someone to do almost anything for you. Here's a list of the kind of help you may need for an event you're organising. It's by no means a definitive list, but I'm including it to give you an idea of the wide range of services on offer. The bigger (or more formal) the event, the more experts you'll need. For a useful list of resources, see the section at the end of this book.

PRE-EVENT

A party planner/organiser: they can look after the whole event for you – as long as your budget can take it! From finding a venue to sending out invitations and hiring other professionals, like a caterer and waiting staff. They can take responsibility for the whole event if you want them to. Advisable for large work functions.

Someone to create/make

Invitations

Special occasion cake (e.g. wedding/birthday)

Goody bags to give guests on leaving

FOR THE ACTUAL DAY

An events/venue/banqueting manager: if you hire a venue, such as a room in a hotel, this person is your point of contact. If your venue is less formal, make sure you still have one person who is in charge of your event and keeping you, the client, happy.

Coat check/meet and greet staff: the first people your guests will see at a large or formal function. Can take names, show guests to tables and give general info on venue's facilities, such as the toilets or telephones.

Caterer/chef/cook: some will come into your home and cook in your kitchen.

Silver service staff: to dish up at formal sit-down affairs.

Florist: can either provide displays for you to place in situ, or for larger or more formal functions may come into your venue and 'dress' it.

Interior designer/decorator: can make your venue look more special or help create a theme for your party.

DJ/musicians/band: every kind of music you can imagine, catering for any event from the very formal to the informal.

Bar/waiting staff: to mix and serve drinks and hand them round at parties.

Photographer: styles and specialities can vary widely.

Cleaning staff: you may want to consider paying someone to look after this side of things. Also discuss if they'd take down any decorations and generally get the venue back in order once the event is over.

THE BASIC RULES OF HIRING STAFF

Whoever it is you're hiring, there are some general rules you should adhere to to make sure you get what you want. They're mostly common sense, but you'd be amazed how many people skip them. Don't be one of those people! You'll be wasting your money.

DECIDE WHAT YOU WANT

What kind of party are you throwing? If you need a caterer, are you looking for someone to prepare hot or cold food? Buffet or sitting down? If you want a photographer, do you prefer posed or reportage-style pictures? Colour or black and white? The more specific you are about your needs, the higher your chances of getting what you want. Take inspiration from any other parties you've been to, look in magazines, jot down ideas. The more input you can have the better.

The danger involved in hiring a professional is holding the party *they* think you should have, rather than the one you want. Of course, you don't have to have it all worked out before you approach a professional. A good, experienced person will relish helping you firm up your ideas by offering suggestions or showing you examples of their past work. But what you *must* make sure of is that before any work commences, you are both agreed on what is required.

FIND THE RIGHT PERSON FOR THE JOB

Again, knowing the style of party and the mood you want to create will help you immensely in finding the right expert. If you want flowers for a very formal affair, for example, there's no point going to a trendy, avant-garde florist. Ask friends, neighbours and colleagues for personal recommendations. Perhaps you attended a party recently where the flowers/food/music were particularly good. Can the host give you the relevant telephone number?

If you can't get a personal recommendation, then do your research. Look in the phone directory or on the Internet and try local firms and people first (they'll be cheaper and are often just as good). Failing that, try any professional bodies or guilds for contacts of, say, photographers or florists in your area. Go along to their premises and get a feel for their work.

SAMPLE THEIR WARES

Reputable people will have a portfolio of photographs or samples of their work. Ask for personal references (take them up yourself, rather than accepting a letter they hand you), or in the case of a band, watch a video of them performing. Ask as many questions as you want. If you get a bad gut feeling about someone or a company, or they don't return calls quickly, listen to those alarm bells and go elsewhere. Do spend time shopping around.

COMMUNICATE WHAT YOU WANT

Show them any ideas you've had and spend some time discussing what's required. Ask them if they're able to do it. Have they done this kind of thing before? When? Can you speak to the client concerned to get a reference? Don't be shy about this; it's standard procedure with true professionals and anyone worth their salt will not take offence. If they seem on a different wavelength to you, find someone who is more in tune with your style. Don't be swayed into creating a party that is too far from what you really want. That said, do listen to any professional advice about what is actually possible. If they say it's a bad idea to try to cook a three-course meal for twenty in your tiny kitchen, they're telling the truth.

MAKE A DECISION

Get a price in writing from at least two or three companies before making your decision. Check that the price includes all taxes, any service charges/transport costs, or other hidden extras. Go with people you like the most and who inspire the most confidence.

AGREE ON THE NITTY-GRITTY

Detail is everything. Get the following agreed and in writing before proceeding:

Time of their arrival and departure.

How they need the venue/area set up and who will do it.

What they will provide in the way of services and equipment.

What you will provide.

Will they need to be fed during the evening?

Will they take breaks? What happens then?

Any restrictions at all (e.g. can your DJ play CDs? Will your barperson serve spirits? Can your guests smoke in the venue you've hired?)

Have they checked out the venue for suitability? Any potential problems?

What will they wear? This may be an issue for more formal affairs if they're on show.

GET A CONTRACT! GET A RECEIPT!

Anything you agree should be put in writing, and you should be given a receipt for any deposit you pay. Smaller companies may shirk from contracts. Type one up yourself that simply states what they've agreed to do, and the price you've agreed to pay for it, get them to sign it, you sign it and keep a copy each. If they don't want to do this, go elsewhere.

THE SPECIFIC RULES OF HIRING STAFF

Here are the areas you may want to think through when hiring specific people. It's not an exhaustive list, but it is a good start.

HIRING A COOK/CHEF/CATERER

→ Agree on what they will cook (and whether you or they will provide ingredients and equipment).
→ Agree on where the cooking will take place. If it isn't their own kitchen, make sure they see the venue well before the day.
→ Have a taste! If you haven't already attended a party they've catered for, get them to do a 'tasting' for you once you've agreed on the menu. This gives you a chance to eliminate anything you don't like and choose between options. This is standard procedure, though you may be charged for this. A tasting session should include any wine you'll be serving, too.

→ Discuss any guests' allergies and food intolerances.
→ Make it clear if you need them to serve the food, too, or if you'll be providing waiting staff. If it's the latter, get the two parties to talk to each other before the day so the waiting staff know exactly what's being served when and what's in it (they're bound to be asked). Some caterers can provide their own waiting staff.

HIRING A FLORIST

→ For large events, florists will make up examples of the table settings and decorations for you to see beforehand.
→ Make sure the florist is providing everything (e.g. any candles you may want in your arrangements, etc.).
→ When will they need to get into the venue to set up?
→ What will they do if the flowers they want to use aren't available on the day? Have a plan B unless they are 100 per cent certain there will be no problem.
→ If you're having a bouquet for a wedding, be clear about the size you want. See an example. Many a gorgeous bride has been swamped by a huge triffid-like arrangement.

HIRING A VENUE

→ How often do they run the kind of event you want at this venue? Can you speak to past clients?
→ Make sure your guests know how to get there. Supply a map (the venue may be able to give you ready-printed ones) and include the venue's contact details. Ideally this should go out with the invitations.
→ Check on accessibility for any disabled guests.
→ Check on whether children are allowed. If so, and your guests are parents, ensure it's a child-friendly environment, with mother & baby facilities as well as high chairs, if needed.
→ Research local B&Bs if guests will have to stay over, and also make sure you have a few numbers of cab companies for departing guests.
→ Do you have to use the suppliers provided by the venue or can you use your own (some venues do not allow you to bring your own caterer)?
→ Find out if red wine is allowed (some venues don't allow it because of the possibility of staining their carpets/linens).
→ Is dancing allowed? (Some venues don't want heels on their parquet flooring.)
→ Is smoking allowed?
→ What time will you be allowed in and what time will you have to vacate?
→ How many people fit into the room? Seated or standing?

→ Is there an area to welcome guests? Will there be a sign/person directing them to your party?

→ Can you have a separate drinks area before dinner?

→ How long will the licence for alcohol run?

→ Are decorations allowed and when can you have access to put them up? By when do you need to take them down (and clear up)?

→ Who will set up the room? (Will you be expected to sort out place cards, for example, or is there a member of staff who can do this for you?) Be absolutely certain you know who is doing what on the day, so you don't find you're left folding napkins as guests arrive.

→ Any restrictions on music? What power supply do they have? (Get your musician/DJ to pay a visit.)

→ Check the toilet facilities. Are there enough?

→ If your event is an evening one, visit it during the night so you can see what it will be like.

(For ideas on the kinds of venues for hire, see Chapter 1.)

HIRING A MUSICIAN/BAND/DJ

→ Venues can recommend musicians (they often get a commission for doing this). Do still check them out for yourself before agreeing to hire them. Can they provide music for the kind of event you want? Don't get a wedding band for your nephew's 16th birthday. He won't thank you.

→ See videos of them in action or go along and hear them play.

→ Be specific about the kind of music you want and ask if they can provide it. If there's a type of music you *don't* want, tell them.

→ Can they provide lights for the disco or band, and is there adequate power at the venue?

(For more information on music at parties, see Chapter 8.)

HIRING A PHOTOGRAPHER

→ Tell them the style of photo you want and show examples. Are they the right person for the job?

→ Ask to see any examples similar to your description. If they have none, go elsewhere. You don't want someone experimenting on your event as you won't be able to recreate it!

→ Be specific about whether you want colour or black and white film, and roughly how many rolls you want taken.

→ Give the photographer a list of any particular groupings you want photographed together (e.g. bride and her sisters; the in-laws; colleagues and the couple).

→ Assign someone to the photographer who knows the other guests, give them a duplicate list, and ask them to point out who everyone is.
→ Get the photographer to check out the venue, lighting etc., and bring along any equipment for every weather eventuality.
→ Agree on when you'll see proofs of the photos, cost of prints, size and delivery date.

AND IF YOU REALLY CAN'T AFFORD THE PROFESSIONALS...

... call in your friends. Most of us know a fantastic cook, great cocktail-maker, budding photographer, enthusiastic amateur DJ. Ask if they'd mind helping out for your event. If they have a real talent, chances are they really enjoy it, too, and will feel flattered to be asked. Explain what you want, and buy them a gift as a thank you once the event is over. And, of course, do give them some help on the day and make sure they're well looked after so they don't feel like they're missing out. Do be appreciative, don't expect professional standards, and be gracious if it doesn't quite go according to plan. After all, they're doing you a massive favour. It goes without saying that you shouldn't use friends for very important events, like weddings. It's too big a risk.

For smallish events held in your house, don't forget to make use of your local deli or gourmet store. Many shops will prepare and deliver wonderful food ready for eating. It's a good way of serving something special without having to go to the effort of cooking it yourself, and is quite acceptable for a buffet.

YOUR FIVE-MINUTE CHECKLIST

→ Plan, plan, plan. The more you're spending, the more people involved, the more that can go wrong. Be meticulous in your planning, start early and communicate well and you'll pull off an amazing event.
→ Decide what you want then find the right person for the job.
→ Check out references, sample their work and hammer out details.
→ Get everything in writing, including a contract and prices.
→ Be open to suggestions, but don't be bullied into doing something completely different if you don't want to.

MISTAKES TO AVOID

MY COUSIN'S NEIGHBOUR'S DENTIST USED THIS GREAT DJ – I'LL GIVE HIM A TRY.

That's fine if you don't mind taking a big risk. Even with personal recommendations, it's still a good idea to check out the person yourself. After all, if you get it wrong there is no going back. And you can bet your cousin's neighbour's dentist has a very different taste to you in music.

LOOK, I JUST WANT SOME NICE NIBBLY THINGS – SURPRISE ME!

Don't make me laugh. Surprises are the last thing you want. Be specific, be focused and be clear on what you're asking for. You wouldn't go into a restaurant and ask for 'something hot and yummy' would you? If you really don't know what you want, ask what's on offer and talk it through with the professional. They can give good advice on what works well, but only you know your guests (and, er, their food allergies...)

EXPERT, SHMEXPERT – I'LL DO IT MYSELF!

Great idea in theory. But how are you going to feel about blowing up a hundred balloons on the morning of your wedding, or fiddling around with filigree when you should be having your first drink and welcoming your guests? The beauty of hiring a professional is that it leaves you to enjoy yourself. If money's an issue, scale down your event before going down the DIY route.

PART TWO: PUTTING IT INTO PRACTICE

12 HOW TO THROW A COCKTAIL PARTY

Who could resist an invitation to a cocktail party? There's something decidedly decadent about sipping Kir Royales with friends, or shaking up Martinis in your kitchen. Most people love the idea of a cocktail party because it just seems so glamorous. Ask your guests to dress up, and you could almost be in a Bond movie.

But don't be fooled. As the host, cocktail parties can be a huge amount of work, and unless you get the planning right you're likely to spend all evening frantically rinsing out glasses, spearing olives and slicing lemons. Which, of course, defeats the purpose of inviting people into your home in the first place.

WHAT KIND OF PARTY?

If it's your first time, keep it simple. The most common mistake people make when hosting a cocktail party is trying to do too much by offering too wide a range of drinks. Your friends don't expect you to have the skills of Tom Cruise in *Cocktail* – they've turned up to see you, have a good time, try out a few drinks, and enjoy themselves – so don't put yourself under unnecessary pressure.

If you theme your party it helps cut down on choice and can make the whole thing a lot easier to manage. Try a Margarita party, for example, a Martini party or a champagne cocktail party (no shaking needed, easy). Let guests know you'll be serving other drinks, too, (keep a few bottles of wine and non-alcoholic drinks in reserve) so they don't turn down your invitation because they happen to hate your choice of cocktails.

Also think about the time of day for your party. Traditionally, cocktail parties were held pre-dinner, between the hours of 4 p.m. and 7 p.m. That doesn't mean you have to follow suit. You may decide to make it a post-dinner party, starting at, say, 8.30, so guests arrive having eaten and you supply just a few nibbles. Your party can start whenever you want. State on your invitation when the party will end, so guests have an idea. A self-contained, early evening affair is a good way to start out if you haven't done this before. It means you won't get exhausted, nobody will get too drunk and you'll leave them wanting more. For tips on how to wind down a party and get guests to leave, see Chapter 9.

How formal do you want your party to be? If you'd like your guests to dress up to give the event a sense of occasion, let them know. Make sure they understand what you mean by 'dress up'. Think about what kind of atmosphere you'd like to create. You might just want a funky drinks party for all your friends, a slightly smarter 'no jeans' affair, or you may want to go for broke and ask guests to wear evening dress and black tie. Younger people tend to be put off by dress codes so you might want to take that into consideration. You know your friends and how they're likely to react (though be warned that the more upmarket you make it and the more effort they put in, the higher their expectations will be).

Even if you are having an informal, small gathering, sending out invitations rather than phoning or emailing guests is preferable. You want people to know this is a special event. See Chapter 2 about invitations.

For a first-time cocktail party, it's best to keep it fairly informal and numbers small (12–20 maximum) to help you, the host, feel more relaxed too. If you do need it to be more formal (say if it's a wedding party or a special anniversary) try calling in the professionals (see Chapter 11) and consider hiring a venue, too.

COST

The general assumption is that throwing a glamorous cocktail party is an expensive way to entertain. That isn't necessarily so. There's a lot you can do to cut costs without looking like you're cutting corners.

The best way to stay within your budget is to decide on which drinks you'll be serving and stick to a limited bar list. If your event is among friends and less formal, ask guests who accept your invitation to bring a specific drink each. So, for example, you may decide you want to serve Kir Royales, Bellinis, Champagne

Cocktails, Long Island Iced Tea, Martinis, Bloody Marys and Margaritas.

Buy a few bottles of champagne to start with, so while early guests arrive, you can make the Kir Royales, Bellinis and Champagne Cocktails easily (they require no shaking, so will give you a chance to mingle and introduce people).

Then as the party really gets going and your other guests arrive, your bar will gradually get stocked up. Ask them to bring vodka, gin, tequila, Cointreau, vermouth, more champagne (or Cava – depending on how much of a purist you are and how rich your friends are). Only do this if your friends are reliable and you know they will definitely turn up – you don't want to jeopardise your party because someone couldn't be bothered to show. If someone RSVPs with a 'maybe', ask them to bring something that isn't crucial, like another bottle of Cava. Guests don't have to bring standard-sized bottles of spirits, quarts will do. And if you do run out, simply make something else. You supply soft drinks: peach juice (for Bellinis), angostura bitters and sugar cubes (for Champagne Cocktails), cola (Long Island Iced Tea). With this 'bring a bottle' system, you'll be surprised how much alcohol you'll have left over at the end of the party!

Make life easy and buy ready-prepared bottles of Bloody Mary mix and Margarita mix. You can get these easily, they taste great, and all you need to do is supply the salt-rimmed glasses for the Margaritas and the celery, tabasco and Worcestershire sauce for the BMs. Pour the mixes into jugs before the party starts.

ICE

Probably as important as the alcohol, make sure you have much more ice than you think you'll need. You can buy bags of ice from off-licences or supermarkets. If you have no room in your freezer, keep ice in a sink or fill the bath, and make sure all your drinks that need chilling (like champagne and soft drinks) are already cold. You'll also need ice for adding to drinks, crushing into Margaritas and for shaking cocktails (some cocktails are shaken with ice, poured through the shaker and the ice discarded). You'll be getting through a lot of it, so make sure you have plenty of ice. For a party of twenty, that includes shaken, iced cocktails, and lasts from 8–12, I'd get about four large bags. In summer you'll get through more than in winter. A portable cold box (like the kind you take on a picnic) is perfect for storing cold beer, wine and soft drinks. If it's a casual party, it's fine for this to be visible, with a label on top telling guests what's inside and to help themselves.

EQUIPMENT

→ Get yourself a **cocktail shaker** – unless you're planning to serve just champagne. They're not expensive, easy to use and look great. Everyone will want to have a go. A standard shaker comprises a base, a strainer and a cap. The Boston Shaker comprises one glass and one steel shaker. You place the ingredients in the glass, put the steel half on top (pressing down with the heel of your hand to create a vacuum), shake holding both ends well (glass part always on top), give the chrome part a knock with your hand to break the vacuum, then pour out your drink using a Hawthorne strainer. As you can see, a standard shaker is by far easier!

→ **Bar measure/shot** – this is a tiny chrome tumbler measure that is vital if you're going to follow any recipe. It comes in a 25ml measure (UK) or a 1oz measure (US).

→ **A good cocktail book** – one of the best is *American Bar* by Charles Schumann (Abbeville Press Publishers, £16.95) and has hundreds of easy-to-use recipes for everything from a classic Martini to a Green Russian (crème de menthe and vodka, in case you were wondering).

→ **A bar spoon** – this is a long-handled spoon that's slightly larger than a standard teaspoon. It's used for stirring drinks with ice. Also good for getting to the bottom of that Margarita jug.

→ **A strainer** – most good shakers come with a strainer built in to the lid. If the recipe requires fine straining to remove pips for example (e.g. Raspberry Martinis) you can use a chrome tea strainer for this, held under the shaker as you pour out the drink. Buy one just for cocktails – you don't want your Martinis tasting of tea!

→ **Chopping board and sharp knife** – for those lemon/lime wedges.

→ **Juicer** – roll lemons and limes on a board first to get more juice out of them.

→ **An ice crusher** – a great contraption that has a compartment for ice, rotating blades and a handle like a big pencil sharpener. It's not essential but is perfect for crushing ice for Margaritas and Caiparinhas. You might want to get one if you decide to make cocktail parties a way of life.

WHICH GLASSES?

There are thirteen styles of glasses but you need only bother with a few (after all, how often are you called upon to mix a hot toddy?) The types of glasses you need depend on which drinks you're going to serve – another good reason to keep it simple.

A Martini *must* be served in a Martini glass (a 'V' shaped, stemmed glass, also called a cocktail glass). If you want Margaritas, you'll need a 'coupette' – a Margarita glass with a large rim for rubbing lime on then dipping in salt. (Margarita salt is a special salt you can buy from outlets that stock the mix – it's not ordinary table salt!). A tall glass (or a Collins/Highball glass) is invaluable for long drinks like Long Island Iced Tea, or non-alcoholic drinks. And a short glass with a heavy base – an Old Fashioned – is great if you want to serve Scotch or any spirits straight. Make sure you have some standard wine glasses around, too.

A FLUTE OR A SAUCER?

Champagne saucers have fallen out of favour with mixologists (as some barpeople now like to be called) as they allow the bubbles to disappear too quickly. Flutes are much more widely used now for champagne cocktails. If you're not too bothered about bubbles and are simply going for effect, champagne saucers win every time. They're far more glamorous and add a certain Hollywood touch.

BUT I'VE ONLY GOT FOUR GLASSES

Don't panic. If you don't have these glasses – and few people do – you can hire them from off-licences and party organisers easily. If you're buying alcohol from these outlets, they often allow you to borrow the glasses for free – you return them the next day. It's worth hiring glasses if you're having a reasonably large party. Don't forget that people may put their glasses down and lose them or change drinks several times during a party so make sure you have more glasses than guests. A bit of rinsing glasses as you go along isn't a bad idea but you don't want to be stuck at the sink up to your elbows in suds all night. This book has very few strict rules, but here's one of them: under *no* circumstances should you serve cocktails in plastic cups. Save them for picnics.

WRITING YOUR COCKTAIL RECIPES

Forget scrabbling around in your recipe book every time someone orders a Long Island Iced Tea. This is a foolproof way to mix cocktails quickly and expertly.

1. Decide what you will be offering.

2. Take one sheet of paper and type or write down the name of each cocktail, plus how to make it. Write on it what kind of glass you need and any garnishes that might be vital to the drink. This is your crib sheet. Pin it somewhere near your bar (a kitchen cupboard, for example, but not on a work surface as you're bound to spill something on it).

3. Before your guests arrive, make a bar list so they know what's on offer. This is a bit like a menu they'd get in a restaurant. This can be anything from a simple typewritten or written out piece of card to something a bit more special. If you want to get fancy, take some black paper or card and fold, so it opens out like a book. Inside, with a silver pen, write down the names of the cocktails (plus a short description of the ingredients). Have some fun with it, give your bar a name and write it on the front of the bar list. I had a party a few years ago where we called our kitchen the Titanic Bar and renamed all the cocktails accordingly. Make a few duplicate bar lists so guests can pass them round amongst themselves.

4. One of the best things about cocktail parties is deciding what to try next. Once your guests arrive, the bar lists will help add a sense of excitement to the occasion. When someone has chosen what they'd like, refer to the crib sheet that's pinned up above the bar and make it for them.

PREPARING THE BAR

Planning is everything when it comes to entertaining, but it's particularly important for a successful cocktail party as there are so many elements involved. Clear as much space as possible and lay out the following before guests arrive:

Ice (preferably in a bucket, and more on standby)

Ice crusher

Trays of glasses

A couple of tea towels

Any jugs of ready-mixed drinks

All the other drinks you'll need (go through your crib sheet and make sure you have each ingredient within easy reach)

Garnishes: lemon slices/wedges/cocktail olives/celery/Margarita salt in a large saucer. Again, check your crib sheet. Spear those olives for Martinis, make the lemon twists and cut those lime wedges now. It's these details that people love.

Swizzle sticks for stirring (or plastic chopsticks)

Cocktail shaker and shot measure

Bar spoon

Juicer

Strainer (if needed)

Chopping board and knife

Bottle opener/corkscrew

If you have a big kitchen you're lucky. Now you know why it's a good idea to limit your party to just a few types of drinks! The mixing of the drinks is a crucial part of the party, and is really what it's all about, so don't be surprised if everyone ends up congregating near the bar person as they work their magic.

WHAT? I HAVE TO SERVE FOOD, TOO?

Even though guests won't be expecting food, you really should serve a few nibbles, if for no other reason than to stop everyone drinking so fast. It's bad form to serve drinks with nothing at all, and you'll end up with a roomful of ill people on your hands.

The kind of food you serve depends on how formal the party is, but assuming it's casual, you're fine with some posh crisps, cocktail sausages, a few crudités and other finger food. Later on in the evening, bring out a bowl full of fun-size chocolate bars or something else sweet as most people will fancy a sweet bite after all that savoury.

Place bowls or plates of food strategically to encourage people to wander and eat, or get a friend to help you pass round trays of snacks. This stops everyone crowding around one table. Supply small cocktail napkins, make sure all food can be eaten with one hand, and don't serve anything that will have pits, bones or any other kind of debris. And don't forget to cater for any vegetarians; use red napkins to line any bowls that contain meaty nibbles, and let them know on arrival. Or put a small card next to meaty food, like a name place card, so guests can see for themselves.

If you're going for a more sophisticated party, you may want to call in at your local deli for ready-prepared nibbles, or even hire a caterer to provide for you (see Chapter 11). The last thing you want to do is to spend ages cooking. A cocktail party is hard work, and if you decide to do lots of cooking you'll be shattered before it even starts. And anyway, the emphasis at a party like this is really on the drinks and the sociability of it all – and everyone understands that.

SOME FAVOURITE COCKTAILS FROM THE SAVOY'S AMERICAN BAR

The famous American Bar, at London's Savoy Hotel, has attracted personalities from the worlds of cinema, theatre, politics and business for over a century now. Here head barman, Peter Dorelli, shares some of the most popular cocktails they serve today. (1 shot = 25ml)

DRY MARTINI

A simple classic that, when served correctly, is still the best

Freeze the gin (to thicken slightly)

Pour 75ml into a frozen glass

Add a dash of vermouth

Place a twist of lemon peel on top and serve

COSMOPOLITAN

After the Dry Martini, this is the most popular cocktail currently served

2 shots vodka

1 shot Cointreau

1½ shots cranberry juice

½ shot of lime juice

Dash of egg white

Shake ingredients together and serve with a wedge of lime

WHITE LADY

This cocktail is one of The Savoy's own creations

50ml gin

25ml Cointreau

25ml lemon juice

Dash of egg white

Shake ingredients together and serve garnished with a cherry

SEA BREEZE

50ml vodka

25ml grapefruit juice

25ml cranberry juice

Pour ingredients over ice and decorate with a wedge of lime

13 ROMANTIC DINNER FOR TWO

Inviting someone round for a romantic dinner is the oldest seduction technique in the book. And, hey, it works! Or it can do if handled carefully. The fact is, someone isn't going to fall in love with you, or agree to jump into bed just because you've rustled up a meal. But cooking for someone shows that you care enough to make the effort, and when it's one-on-one everyone understands the subtext. It's not really about the food at all. It's about spending time with that person, getting to know them better and, well, do I really need to spell it out?

Dinner for two is also an excellent opportunity for your guest to get to know you by coming into your home and watching you play host. How you pitch the evening and present yourself and your home will tell them more about you than your conversation ever could. In situations like these, when we're trying to second-guess each other, the unspoken stuff, like the mood of the event and the atmosphere we create is particularly important.

'OH, IS IT JUST *ME*?'

It's *very* important your guest knows that they will be the *only* guest. It's dishonest (and mean) to spring it on them when they arrive that, actually, it's just the two of you having a cosy night in. (Happened to me once – not nice. I turned up straight from work, expecting a casual dinner with half a dozen people. My host stood in the doorway dressed as if he was about to go to the opera, champagne glass in hand. It took great self-control not to bolt.)

Of course you can have a one-on-one dinner with a friend that's purely platonic. And if you both understand that romance isn't on the menu, then that makes life easier. But if you are planning a little romance, the two most important tips are to keep the evening simple and keep it relaxed. Don't go for formality or you'll scare them off. Obviously you want to look like you've made an effort, but not *too* much of an effort, otherwise they'll think you're stalker material. You don't want to seem desperate, but also beware of appearing so laid-back that it looks like you're not that bothered that they even turned up. You've already declared your interest by inviting them. Here's how to have a great evening.

AMBIENCE IS EVERYTHING

The food matters at a dinner for two, but more important is the ambience you create. This will say a great deal about your intentions, so make sure you get it right! A relaxed, warm, informal atmosphere should put you both at ease. Again, it's about striking a balance between making an effort and keeping it homely. If you're celebrating a special event – a birthday or anniversary – or you're already in a relationship with the person you're entertaining, you can afford to pull out the stops and go a bit more formal. If, however, it's a first date or getting-to-know-you event, formality will make them (and you) nervous. There are other ways of impressing him/her other than resorting to elaborate table settings or very posh food.

LIGHTING

Yes, it's a cliché, but candlelight really does the trick here, as it creates a feeling of intimacy and cosiness. Plan your lighting beforehand and try it out, so you're not rushing around trying to get the right combination when your guest has arrived.

Start the evening with a soft light from side lamps or uplighters, or failing that with dimmed lights (not too low or you'll freak them out as soon as they walk in). You may want to progress onto the dimmed lights, once you've had your meal and are at the coffee stage of the evening. If you have a good selection of lighting it's possible to be flexible and change the mood of the evening quite easily. Obviously, the aim is to make the mood change appear seamless and spontaneous, not meticulously timed.

CANDLES

If I only went for one lighting 'trick' during a romantic dinner, it would be candles grouped on or near the dinner table. Make sure you can see what you're eating and each other. If the candlelight isn't strong enough, use a side light, too, but keep it away from the table so it's not intrusive but still gives you light. Steer away from scented candles on the dinner table, as the aroma will interfere with your sense of smell and taste. If you want to use scented candles, have them in the lounge where you either start the evening with drinks or end it with coffee. Candles needn't be expensive – bags of tea lights are very cheap and, if grouped together or used in little lanterns, can have a dramatic effect.

Of course, if using candles, always make sure you're in the room and keep an eye on them throughout the evening. Never let them burn right through or you run the risk of damaging your furniture as well as setting the place alight. That's not the kind of impression you're after. It's always a good idea to place them on a pretty coaster or some other surface where their heat can't damage your furniture. Be particularly careful of any nearby curtains, flowers and napkins.

FAIRY LIGHTS

If you want to create a very special, stylish feel to the evening you can't go wrong with fairy lights. Drape them across a mantelpiece or over a large potted plant. You should be able to use your fairy lights over and over again so, it's worth paying for good quality ones that will last for years. I love them because they are a very simple way of creating a real sense of occasion. They create a magical ambience and are perfect if your romantic dinner is a celebration for a special birthday or an anniversary. Perhaps for a first-date dinner they may seem a little *too* special, but it's really up to you. Unlike candles, of course, once lit you don't need to keep an eye on them. For more tips on lighting, see Chapter 5.

USING FLOWERS

Flowers are evocative and, apart from the scent, are beautiful to look at. Women, in particular, love flowers, so if you're male and you've asked a woman round for dinner, you could do much worse than having a few carefully chosen stems in a vase. For a more modern arrangement, choose either just one type of flower or contrast two colours. Avoid highly-scented blooms at the dinner table and keep all flowers below eye level so they don't interfere with that all-important eye contact.

Of course, flowers don't need to be kept to the dinner table. You can have vases around the house or sitting in an empty, unused fireplace. Play around with shapes and sizes and experiment with where you place containers.

If you know very little about flowers, don't despair. There are no real rights and wrongs, just go for the ones that appeal to you. Chances are, if you like them they will also fit in with the rest of your decor at home. As a general rule, the more stylised the flower, the more contemporary the feel (gerberas, lilies, iris). Flowers that have rounder petals and a softer, more cottagey look, such as open roses, peonies and hydrangeas will look more romantic and old-fashioned. For advice on buying flowers and which kind of blooms suit which containers, see Chapter 5.

YOUR TABLE SETTING

How formal you make this really depends on the note you want to strike, but I would err on the side of informal when it comes to a romantic dinner. The fact that you've invited your guest by themselves, that you've lit a few candles and have some great, relaxed music playing should really say it all. By all means go for a tablecloth and matching napkins if you like, but I think a small vase of flowers and a few candles are more likely to put your guest at ease than starched table linen. Think about your crockery, cutlery and glasses beforehand and make sure they're clean and to hand. Some nice, thick paper napkins are probably OK to use here (rather than pieces of torn off kitchen roll!).

If your romantic dinner is for a long-standing partner, you might want to dress the table to make it feel different from all the other meals you share together. In which case, go to town with a number of ideas: use strips of beautiful sari fabric instead of a tablecloth; bring ivy or honeysuckle in from the garden and drape across the table/mantelpiece, or use fairy lights in the same way; throw some rose petals over the table. Have fun with it – the possibilities are endless, and you can find more ideas in Chapter 5.

GETTING THE MUSIC RIGHT

Music is a vital ingredient in setting any scene, and is probably one of the most important factors during a romantic dinner. Think about the music beforehand and plan what you'd like to play. Obviously, stay flexible if your guest requests anything else, but don't spend ages rummaging through your music collection once your guest has arrived. Do you know what kind of music they like? Find out. For a romantic dinner you want something reasonably low key and not too obviously 'smoochy'. Forget anything with explicit lyrics please! Try some instrumental music, or one of the excellent 'chill out' compilations you can buy. As the evening progresses, change the music to suit the mood (or match it). But try not to be a bore, and don't make it too contrived. You're aiming for an easy, elegant kind of feel to the evening – not a function that's been planned with military precision.

THE FOOD

Oh, what to cook? You want to impress him/her but not look like you're desperate. And then there's the small matter of your limited culinary skills. Two rules to keep in mind: keep it simple, keep it relaxed. Even if you're a great cook, fussy food will create a formal atmosphere. S/he hasn't come here to eat (well, not really) s/he's come here to check you out, see what s/he thinks of you and find out if this could go further. The food plays a supporting role, and *you* are the main attraction. Of course it has to be edible and that's why you have to be honest with yourself regarding your skills. What can you manage well?

'With a romantic dinner, think about the tastes and textures,' says Charlotte Butterworth, party creator at Create Food (a bespoke catering company). 'It may sound corny, but try to think of some food that you can share – like spears of asparagus with a frothy hollandaise sauce, lobster claws with saffron aoli. And always choose food that doesn't take too much time to prepare, like smoked salmon.'

BEFORE YOU PLAN YOUR MENU, CONSIDER THE FOLLOWING:

→ Is s/he veggie or does s/he have any food dislikes/allergies/intolerances? Find out.

→ Avoid messy or fiddly food (e.g. spaghetti, anything that creates a lot of debris, like serving a whole poussin each, or fish on the bone).

→ Avoid heavy food. Go for something light and fresh. You want to feel energised after dinner, not half asleep – especially if you're hoping the night will develop. I'd go for chicken or fish, as red meat can be very filling. If you really want to serve red meat, aim for small portions.

→ Choose recipes that you've tried before (successfully!) and know you can handle. If you have not tried anything before, have a practice run in the days leading up to the dinner.

→ Do your flavours work well together? If you're having something cheesy as a starter, do you really want a cheese sauce on your main course too?

→ Choose food that can be prepared beforehand and needs very little last-minute attention. This is very important as you have only invited one guest. If you're in the kitchen who are they going to talk to? If you're a supremely confident cook, of course, you can invite them to watch you prepare the food, though I don't know anyone who actually likes cooking in front of their guests.

CAN I GET AWAY WITH COOKING A READY MEAL?

Well, to a point. But frankly, your date could get one of those at home. If you're very short of time or simply can't cook, you can serve a ready meal, but you *must* make some effort with it and customise it. For example, if you buy a fresh soup for a starter, sprinkle on some shaved parmesan or other garnishes. Bake some pre-prepared frozen bread rolls to go with it. You need to give it a home-made twist to show that you are willing to put a bit of effort in.

Terry Farr, award-winning chef patron of Friends restaurant in Pinner, England, says, 'At a romantic dinner, I'm sure your guest would appreciate a bit of effort going into the meal. If you must go for ready meals, try cooking the main dish yourself and just buying the sauce or veg to go with it. Keep it simple and serve something like a piece of chicken, and cook it yourself. In the fullness of time, if the relationship *is* going to go somewhere, it won't make much difference.'

The problem with ready meals is that they often taste processed and are very salty. And by the time you've scooped them out of the foil tray (you *were* planning on doing that, right?) they look nothing like the picture on the box. If you must go down this route, go for what's known as the 'premium' range in supermarkets. They usually come in silver boxes with fancy italic writing. These meals use better ingredients than your standard ready meal and, of course, cost more. Accompany with a bit of effort – a salad using home-made dressing, or some oven roasted potatoes. A friend tells me the worst romantic dinner she had was when a man served her duck soup (whatever that is), Findus crispy pancakes, followed by Angel Delight – which he insisted was homemade mousse.

Do investigate your local deli where good quality prepared food can be bought. A good deli will sell meals that have a 'home-made' feel to them. If you add your own touches, even better.

CLEVER SHORT CUTS

There *are* ways of saving time that are perfectly acceptable and will be invisible to your guest. In the supermarket look out for:

→ **Ready peeled and washed vegetables**
→ **Ready chopped and washed salad**
→ **Chopped garnishes**
→ **Sauces for pasta, curry, just about everything**
→ **Half-baked bread/rolls you can finish off in the oven**
→ **Don't buy ready grated parmesan (it's tasteless and smells terrible). Get a block of the real thing – it keeps for ages. Create parmesan shavings by using a potato peeler.**

IF YOU'RE COOKING FOR A WOMAN

Avoid anything that involves lots of bones or any other generally messy food that can be embarrassing to eat. If you're having fish, don't leave the head on. And don't cook too much food, but always have a dessert, preferably something chocolatey. It's a cliché, but few women hate chocolate.

IF YOU'RE COOKING FOR A MAN

Don't try making his 'favourite' thing that his mother's been cooking for twenty odd years. You're on a slippery slope here, as you cannot compete with his mother (and shouldn't even bother trying). Avoid nursery food like toad in the hole, mash, pies, etc., and forget that old cliché that a way to his heart is through his stomach. It isn't – it's through his shirt . . .

RECIPE IDEAS

Starter: try something light and fresh. Good quality vine-ripened tomatoes, peppery salami and some buffalo mozzarella. All sliced on a pretty platter, with fresh ciabatta (heat it in the oven beforehand for a just-baked feel).

Main course: ready-marinaded tuna, quickly seared on a griddle or lemon chicken (chicken with lemon quarters, roasted in the oven, with potatoes). Serve with a green salad.

Dessert: seasonal fruit salad. Dilute a couple of teaspoons of white sugar in a cup of water, in a saucepan, with a cinnamon stick. Once cool, pour over fresh, chopped fruit and place in fridge to chill. Or chocolate brownie (shop-bought, warmed through) served with vanilla ice cream. Grate plain chocolate flakes over the top.

ROMANTIC DINNER CRIB SHEET

→ Work to your abilities and only cook what you know you're good at. Consider delis and supermarkets for shortcuts.

→ Ambience is everything – music, flowers, lighting. Put in a bit of effort.

→ Don't forget yourself! Make sure you have time to get changed, and spruced up a bit before s/he arrives.

→ Keep the food light, fresh and simple.

→ Try not to get too nervous. If they weren't already interested they wouldn't have accepted your invitation, would they?

14 SATURDAY NIGHT DINNER PARTY

Saturday night is a very special night. It's the one night of the week when most people make social plans. It's bang slap in the middle of the weekend, most of us have had the whole day to wind down, and not many of us have to work the next day. Everyone seems to be in a good mood and there's a slight party atmosphere about entertaining on a Saturday night – anything could happen. For many of us it may be the only evening we've actually planned what we're doing.

If you're invited to someone's house for dinner on a Saturday night, you expect something a bit special. We're not necessarily talking a lot of expense, cordon bleu food or stiff formality; you just expect your host to have made a bit of an effort. Which is fair enough really. After all, this is your big night out, right?

Throwing a Saturday night dinner party is an event that you graduate to, once you've tried out hosting a few other events first. If you're not confident in the kitchen or just haven't entertained much before, try cooking a less formal supper with friends on a Friday first. It's difficult not to get caught up in the whole 'specialness' of Saturday and bite off more than you can chew. If you really want to hold your event on a Saturday, but are new to playing host, then have a maximum of four people, including yourself, and make sure they are very good friends. The kind of friends you're not going to feel you have to impress. As hosts, throwing a fantastic, memorable Saturday night dinner party is what we all aspire to.

SETTING THE TONE

Whether you're a guest or a host, Saturday night brings with it high expectations. Obviously it depends on what kind of friends you have and who you decide to invite. But if your friends do a fair amount of entertaining themselves, they'll probably be a bit less forgiving than anyone who never cooks, who'll probably just be grateful that it's edible. It's up to you, as host, to choose your guests carefully and set the tone for the evening when you invite them.

Lizz Clarke is a Dale Carnegie trainer and expert on etiquette, working with major companies in helping their staff network. She says, 'Having matching cutlery, etc., is not as important as having a positive and relaxed atmosphere. Don't get stressed – it's rude and creates a negative energy that impacts on the event.'

If the event is formal and you'd like them to dress up a bit, let them know. If you want to make it a casual buffet and ask them to contribute a dish each, ask them. (Make sure you know what everyone is bringing so you get enough variety.) Maybe you want it to be a Mexican evening, and are planning to serve tortillas that they can fill themselves at the table. Although most people expect a bit of effort on a Saturday night, that doesn't mean it has to be formal. A Mexican evening could be a great excuse to go to town with the decor and music. Don't put all the emphasis on the food. Less formal events, like a DIY Mexican meal, can be good fun as long as people know what to expect. Telling them beforehand also gives people a chance to opt out if they loathe Mexican food!

A friend of mine once had a summer dinner party to celebrate his love of ices and sorbets. Every course included a different ice (yes, you can make savoury ices!). A great idea that worked really well, because his guests all loved them too – and knew beforehand what they were letting themselves in for. For a starter, he served Frozen Stilton Cheese Cream, with crackers, followed by Fresh Tomato and Basil Sorbet with a salad. Dessert was Earl Grey Tea Sorbet. (For recipes, see *Ices: the Definitive Guide*, by Caroline Liddell and Robin Weir (Grub Street, 1995).)

RELAX – IT'S ONLY DINNER!

There's nothing worse than a stressed host who is having a terrible time at their own dinner party. It's guaranteed to ruin the evening. The guests will sense the tension, feel guilty about being the cause of all this 'fuss' and will probably end up with indigestion. It's a bit of a cliché, the idea of the host struggling in the kitchen on the verge of a breakdown, but unfortunately it happens all too often. Why? Usually because the host hasn't given enough thought to planning, or is simply being too ambitious.

These days, dinner parties don't need to be formal affairs. 'The dinner party is constantly changing,' says Charlotte Butterworth, a party creator who oversees whole events at Create Food, a bespoke catering and party design company. 'They used to be very formal but now, thanks to the slam-bam attitude of TV chefs, people are more confident about trying new ideas with food and settings.'

DECIDING WHAT TO COOK

There are lots of tips in Chapter 6 on food, and how to choose what's best to cook. Here's a run down of the basic points you really need to keep in mind for a dinner party.

HOW MANY COMING?

It's a great feeling, throwing your doors open and inviting everyone in your address book, but don't do it. Start small and progress from there. I've been playing host for over a decade and I've never had more than six people to a dinner party, including myself. The main reason is that I want to enjoy it and the more people you invite the more tiring it will be. It's a myth to think that an extra two or three won't make much difference, they will.

Another consideration is space. How much do you have? Can you sit the numbers you want comfortably around the table? Remember that your guests are probably going to be at the table for most of the evening. Aim for cosy rather than cramped. Do you have enough chairs? Plates/glasses/cutlery? Borrow anything you need beforehand or invite fewer people.

Carl Braganza, interiors stylist, says, 'A lot of people get stuck on the whole thing about having matching plates, glasses and so on. But nowadays things are less formal and you can mix it up – it looks fantastic and more individual. Also, in the past, everything was set out on the table with all the appropriate cutlery. You could almost work out what you'd be eating from looking at the place setting. Now it's less formal and far less cutlery is used.'

YOUR BUDGET

Entertaining can be very expensive, especially when you're having a dinner party and are more likely to want to pull out the stops. Think about how much you can afford per head before you make up your menu. Do a rough costing. If it's coming out to too much, rethink your menu. Chapter 3 goes into the detail on budgeting for your event – read it, and I promise you'll be able to afford to throw another dinner party again soon.

Also, think about your time. How much time are you willing to spend in the kitchen? And how much time do you *want* to spend in the kitchen? Your menu will decide it all, so choose your courses carefully and think about preparation (including shopping) and how exactly you're going to fit it all in.

Maybe you're able to spend the previous day preparing, or can you take the Friday afternoon off work to get all the shopping done? More likely, you'll be pushed for time and want to go for shortcuts, so you're not frazzled by the time your guests arrive.

YOUR MENU

1. CHOOSE WHAT YOU KNOW

Make sure your dinner party is a success by choosing to cook dishes that you've tried before. The world's leading chefs wouldn't dream of serving something without having a few practice runs first, to iron out any problems – what makes you think you can wing it? This is the one mistake people make over and over again when entertaining. There are several reasons a recipe can go wrong. Perhaps you haven't used that cookbook before, and don't know if the recipe will work? Once you've made it and tasted it, you may want to customise it to suit your taste. The recipe may call for a few techniques you're not familiar with (for example, filleting a fish, or getting the meat out of a crab). Practice makes perfect. Wouldn't you rather try these out when there's no pressure on you to 'perform'? By all means try new recipes, but on yourself and on your nearest and dearest first. If need be, invite some *very* good friends round and tell them you're trying out a recipe and need a few guinea pigs.

2. CHOOSE WHAT'S IN SEASON

You can get strawberries in December but they'll be tasteless *and* expensive. Good chefs always go for food that's in season. It's cheaper, it makes sense and it's nice to feel that you're following the seasons set by nature. And most foods that are available during a particular season tend to go very well together – think blackberries and apples; strawberries and mangoes; sprouts and parsnips.

3. CHOOSE LOCAL PRODUCE

It always tastes better. And local bakers, butchers, grocers and fishmongers are at risk of disappearing, thanks to huge supermarkets available in practically every town. Yet their produce is often far superior because it's probably fresher. Supermarkets often pick crops well before they're ripe, refrigerate them to keep them that way, then put them on their shelves to ripen. The packaged fish you buy in a supermarket just doesn't compare to the fish you can get at a fishmongers. Go for the best ingredients you can afford. You'll need to do less to them in the kitchen.

4. BALANCE YOUR MENU

Think of the menu as a whole, including the colour, texture, taste. Sounds obvious, but if your starter is a carrot soup, don't have carrots with the main course, too (even if you did buy too many and are trying to use them up). Think about how the meal will taste all together. Using pastry in the starter? Don't have it in the main course, too, or your guests will be too full for dessert. (Of course it's up to you how many courses you go for. Don't feel you have to have a starter, though I'd always recommend something for dessert – it feels special.)

Think about the work your menu entails. Do not make three courses yourself unless you a) are very confident; b) have lots of time on your hands. I always buy the dessert. Making sweet things isn't my strong point, so I don't even try. You can get some wonderful home-made desserts these days from delis, bakers and even supermarkets.

Don't forget that if you have the budget, you can get someone else to come and cook for you. If making an excellent impression is vital and you're really not up to it, consider getting some outside help in. Some caterers will cook in your kitchen then leave you to dish up. (See the Resources chapter at the end for details, plus Chapter 11 on hiring professionals.)

5. HOW MUCH TO COOK?

Aim for 4oz of meat per person and 6oz of veg (see Chapter 6 for details).

6. ALLERGIES ANYONE?

Do check, and also ask if there's anything your guests would rather not eat. If you have vegetarians coming, make something for them or a veggie course that everyone can eat. It is not acceptable to expect them just to eat the salad or veg!

GETTING THE SPACE READY

Make sure you have enough space cleared for your guests, especially in the dining area. Prepare the table and place the chairs at each setting. Get plates, cutlery, glasses and serving dishes out beforehand. Is everything clean and ready? Find the corkscrew and put out the salt and pepper.

If you're lighting candles, make sure they're below eye level at the table so they don't interfere with guests' eye contact. The same goes for flowers. (See Chapter 5 on tips for lighting, flowers and decor.) For Saturday night, it's worth thinking about the table, lighting and decor. It's easily done and, because so few people bother, the effect is always dramatic. Carl says, 'Often people just illuminate the middle of the dinner table, but try illuminating every place setting, or dotting candles along the whole table. It's about creating a twinkling effect and adds to the sense of occasion.'

And don't forget the music! Get a few CDs ready beforehand and make sure you have something relaxing to ease your guests into the evening. 'The wrong music is probably worse than no music,' says William Higham, a marketing and trends consultant who's worked in the music industry for fifteen years. 'Banging Belgian techno may not be the best music to put on when your guests first arrive. Try some easy listening, or a chill-out compilation to start with. You have to pitch the music to the mood.' (See Chapter 8 for tips on choosing the right music for your event.)

GETTING IT ALL READY AT THE SAME TIME

This is the part of entertaining that stresses most people out, and at a Saturday night dinner party it somehow seems more important to 'perform' on cue. Your guests are all seated round the table and are expectant. But people who get the dinner to the table on time, at the same time, are not magicians – they're planners.

Have a schedule and work backwards. It really is simple and the only way to do it. Once you've successfully planned the timing of your event, you will never dream of doing it any other way. The more components to your meal, the more important planning is. After all, who wants to eat hot chicken and cold potatoes? Not even very hungry guests who you've kept waiting an hour.

First decide what time you want to eat. Then work backwards to see what time you need to do everything else. Here's a very simple example that also appears in Chapter 6, where you can find some time-saving tips, too.

To eat the main course at 8 p.m.:

Chicken in oven at 6.30 p.m.

Potatoes in oven at 7 p.m.

Bread in oven at 7.45 p.m.

Veg on at 7.50 p.m.

Heat gravy at 7.50 p.m.

Extras: lemon wedges/herbs

Obviously the more courses, the more complicated the timetable. Writing it all down like this will also help you remember everything. Add on the end of your timetable any garnishes or extras that must also be added at the last minute. I tend to invite guests around 45 minutes before I want to serve dinner. That gives them fifteen minutes to be late and half an hour to have a drink and be introduced to other guests beforehand. Don't ask people to sit down and eat on arrival. Very few people ever arrive dead on time, and it's much more relaxed to feel that you can have a drink and a chat beforehand.

THE DRINK

For a dinner party, I'd kick off by offering guests a glass of champagne on arrival, then open some wine to drink with the meal.

Most people like to drink wine with their meal, but do have non-alcoholic drinks on hand for drivers/non-drinkers, too. Don't force people to drink more than they want to. If someone is drinking more than they expected to, suggest you get them a cab at the end of the evening or that they stay overnight. Don't let them drive home. For details on which wine to serve with which food, and how much drink you'll need, see Chapter 7.

SETTING THE TABLE

You may be a knife-fork-plate kind of person and that's it. (Me too.) In which case you can skip this part. But if you're having a fairly formal dinner party, you may want to know what goes where. If you're determined to do it 'properly', you'll need special cutlery that is appropriate for the course you're eating. In other words, not all knives and forks are the same! Some are for fish, some are for starters and so on. Any large department store will be able to help you.

When setting the table, the basic rule is that the smaller cutlery goes on the outside, is used for the first course, and you work your way in towards the plate. So, for example, the starter knife and fork are always the furthest away from the plate.

On the left:

Starter/first course fork

(Fish fork – if using)

Main course fork

Dessert fork

On the right:

Starter/first course knife

(Fish knife – if using)

Main course knife

Dessert spoon

GLASSES

If you're using different glasses for white and red wine and water, they can be placed in a triangle at the top right of each person's place setting (if the plate were a clock it would be at two o'clock). Personally, I think lots of glasses confuse everyone and I prefer just a wine glass and a larger one for water.

GIVING PEOPLE 'FAVOURS'

These are very trendy at the moment. They're individual little gifts – a bit like a goody bag – that are placed at each guest's table setting. Carl says, 'The idea of giving favours stems from the Italian wedding tradition of handing out five sugared almonds. You can use anything – a tiny parcel of chocolates wrapped in cellophane, or even a pack of garden seeds for a summer tea party.' It's not obligatory of course, but a simple device to make your guests feel extra-special. 'The cutlery, plates and glasses are all about utility. Adding a favour gives the table a sense of fun and they're great ice-breakers.'

DOES IT MATTER WHERE I SIT?

Guests will often ask you where you want them. If you're really going to town on the decor you might have name places at their plates so they know where to sit. But it's likely you won't do that unless it's a special occasion, like a wedding reception. Lizz says, 'Ideally, split up couples.' After all, they probably see enough of each other and like speaking to other guests.

It doesn't have to be as rigid as boy-girl-boy-girl, but do keep people who know each other very well apart otherwise it's easy for them to get into a cliquey conversation that others may not be able to contribute to. If you have any very talkative, extrovert guests, keep them in the middle of the table as they're bound to keep the conversation going. If you put them at one end, the table will divide in two. Do put quiet people and talkative ones together, and don't put two quiet people next to each other.

Needless to say, you're doing all this in an effortless, graceful way that doesn't involve saying things like 'well you talk a lot so you stay in the middle'. Lizz says, 'Be flexible. If a couple of guests are naturally moving together, let it go. To be separated and relocated is irritating and can have a negative impact on the atmosphere you've worked so hard to create.'

And remember, you can only do so much. I do think that once people have accepted an invitation it is, to a certain extent, up to them to have a good time. Most people will make an effort to talk to others and keep the conversation going, so try not to worry about it too much.

WHAT HAPPENS AFTER DINNER?

Entertaining is not just about food. You cannot flop on the sofa once they've finished eating and fall asleep. Think about how you'd like your evening to develop and end. If you want to serve coffee, get the cups ready beforehand on a tray. Put coffee in the cafetière so that all you need to do is pour boiling water in it.

Your dinner party may end up with everyone dancing round your stereo, looking through your old photo albums, singing along to karaoke, slumped on the sofa or playing games. Whichever way it goes, try not to be too rigid in your plans. You may have been desperate to get the karaoke out, but if you sense people aren't up for it, don't force the issue. See what the mood is and take it from there. (For tips on playing games, see Chapter 8.)

SATURDAY NIGHT DINNER PARTY CRIB SHEET

→ Keep the numbers small, and invite only close friends if you're not that confident.

→ Choose food you've made before and know that you can do well. Don't shy away from buying the dessert ready-made or cheating with a few deli pieces.

→ Try to make the decor special – it *is* Saturday night, after all.

→ Plan, plan, plan. Work out your schedule beforehand and time it all. That way you won't keep your guests waiting hours.

→ If the worst happens – you burn the dinner/drop it – try to keep calm. Explain with a smile, get a take-out (you pay) and laugh it off. After all, you're among friends. Good hosts never cry/swear loudly while cooking/throw things. Well, not in front of their guests, anyway . . .

15 A SUNDAY FAMILY BARBECUE

Barbecues are a wonderful way to entertain and can be great fun. They can, however, also involve a lot of hard work and be quite stressful. Don't be fooled into thinking that the informality of the event means you can wing your way through it. In fact, I find BBQs more labour-intensive than many other forms of entertaining, which means that more planning and preparation is needed than usual.

If you're having a family BBQ, you'll probably be cooking for a fairly large number of people that includes various generations and tastes. This always makes entertaining harder as it means you have to think more carefully, making sure everyone will be able to find something they like to eat. Other reasons a BBQ can be stressful is the fact that you are cooking or 'performing' while your guests are watching. (People love to crowd around the BBQ and give advice – every cook's nightmare!) All of this can make you more anxious as to whether it will be cooked properly.

Plus, of course, there's the weather to contend with but no amount of preparation is going to save you from a summer downpour. Keep an eye on the forecast and have a contingency plan in case you have to bring everything indoors. If the weather looks ominous in the morning, do call everyone and let them know it's still going ahead and you'll do it indoors if necessary (under the grill). I'd advise going ahead – you've probably already done most of the hard work by now anyway and spent a reasonable amount of money on the food. Do let people know, though or they may assume you're calling it off. And you could be left with a lot of food on your hands and nobody to eat it.

WHEN DO I START COOKING? WHEN DO I STOP?

BBQs are informal and as such, people like to drop in when they can. It's not like a dinner party where it's rude to arrive an hour later than stipulated. The very nature of the BBQ means that food is 'on the go' (i.e. cooking) for a fairly long period of time, and people return with their plates again and again. Nobody expects everything to be ready at the same time, so don't put yourself under this pressure. When inviting guests, tell them the event is between, say, 1 and 5. You can even tell them what time you think you'll be serving food – say, 'burgers from 1.30 onwards'. That lets them know that if they get there at 4.30, half an hour before the BBQ ends, it's likely there will be little left.

I once spent all my time during a BBQ constantly cooking and hardly had chance to speak to any guests. The mistake I made here was assuming that all the food had to be cooked at once. Faced with a hungry crowd of about thirty or more, I found I just couldn't cook those sausages fast enough! I was cooking and they were eating – it was like a race. I should have cooked a batch of food, let them eat it whilst I also had a break and mingled, then made another batch an hour or so later. It doesn't matter if the meat runs out at some stage during a BBQ. People will simply go on to the salads, bread and snacks.

Another rule when hosting a BBQ is to hold back some food. Any food you put out *will* get eaten. Whether it's the summer atmosphere, the smell of the cooking or being outdoors, it seems that BBQs bring out a big appetite in lots of people. And just because you've made ten chicken breasts and only eight of your guests have arrived, don't assume people will think, 'well, there are another two people to come so I won't have an extra one.' They will.

If all your guests haven't arrived yet, hold some food back. When they do arrive they'll appreciate the fact there's a little bit left for them. Also, it's good to pace the event so people can have a drink, eat a bit, socialise and then come back for more. It makes for a more relaxed atmosphere, which is what BBQs should be all about.

TIME OF DAY?

Most BBQs are held in the afternoon, especially if it's a family event and children are coming, though do consider an evening event if you're inviting just adults. On a balmy summer's night, there's nothing nicer than sitting outdoors and eating a leisurely meal. If you're going for an evening event, make sure you have adequate lighting for cooking, and have some citronella candles alight to ward off the midges. Have some blankets, scarves and wraps on hand for guests in case it gets a bit chilly.

KNOWING WHEN IT'S COOKED – AND OTHER SAFETY TIPS

Most of us have eaten at least one terrible BBQ meal. Burnt on the outside, raw on the inside, badly cooked meat is a health hazard. Here are a few tips to keep in mind:

→ Meat with bones will take much longer to cook (chicken wings, drumsticks, chops). Go for boneless meat if you don't want to spend too long at the BBQ.

→ Keep all cooked meat and raw meat separate, in different containers, and use different utensils for them, otherwise you run the risk of giving your guests a nasty bout of food poisoning.

→ Aim for a hygienic and tidy BBQ. Have all your meat in containers, ready to hit the BBQ. Don't take it straight from the pack to the BBQ, dripping blood on the way! Not only is it unhygienic, your guests are looking on – and are then going to have to eat that.

KNOWING WHAT TO COOK

→ If you have veggies in your group (ask beforehand) make sure you save a space for them on the BBQ that has not had any meat on it. Don't use utensils that have touched meat for turning veggie food, and keep plates and dishes separate. If you are using a disposable BBQ (fairly cheap from most supermarkets), consider buying a separate one for veggies. If warming bread/baps/pitta bread on the BBQ, don't place on top of meat for the same reason.

→ Many people these days avoid eating red meat, but eat chicken. Ask when inviting about dietary preferences. It'll help you gauge how much to buy, too.

IT'S NOT JUST ABOUT MEAT

Nothing is more boring than a barbecue where all that is served is meat, meat, meat. Use your imagination. BBQs are great for cooking whole fish (wrapped in foil first), corn on the cob, peppers, chunks of halloumi cheese, giant tiger prawns, sausages and, of course, burgers.

Think about your guests and what they're likely to eat. If children are coming, ask their parents if they have any specific 'likes'. Most kids love sausages, so provide some finger rolls, ketchup and mustard too so they can make their own hot dogs. If you have elderly relatives coming, don't just serve huge steaks or giant chops – they won't thank you. Elderly people tend to have smaller appetites, so go for some lighter, easily digestible food, like chicken and a few salads. They may also be averse to spicy foods, so keep this in mind.

Don't make food that has to stand on a table for hours in the sun and runs the risk of going bad – like salmon for example, or anything eggy. Make sure all your salads/mayonnaise/dips are well-chilled beforehand, so that they can withstand being out of the fridge for a while. At the end of the BBQ throw away anything that's been standing a long time.

HOW MUCH TO MAKE

Make a good number of different foods that you can prepare beforehand (a pasta salad perhaps, a green salad and a potato salad), but don't try to barbecue too wide a variety of meat. There's no reason you *have* to cook any red meat if many of your guests don't eat it. Instead opt just for chicken and some sausages for the kids. I'd recommend sticking to about three or four different things on the barbecue and no more.

Nobody expects to sample everything. With BBQs the idea of 'portions' go out of the window. Don't feel that everyone has to have one sausage each, one baked potato, one piece of chicken and so on. Make a few of everything and, as long as you have lots of fresh bread and salad, people are happy to just take what's available. Try to be quite relaxed about this otherwise you really will spend all day sweating over the BBQ rather than chatting to your guests. Food should be plentiful but not with too much choice. That way you'll keep an eye on the cost, too. BBQs have the potential to be very expensive, especially if you're buying large amounts of meat.

WHY YOU NEED TO MARINADE

A marinade is a mixture of oil, herbs, garlic, vinegar – whatever you want it to be – that the meat soaks in before it's cooked. If you've ever had beautifully barbecued food, I guarantee it was marinaded beforehand. A marinade works by tenderising the meat, adding flavour and helping it stay lovely and moist while cooking. Meat can easily dry out on a BBQ, but a marinade will make sure it stays juicy and delicious, as well as bringing out depth of flavour. Everything benefits from a marinade – fish, chicken, beef, lamb and prawns. You don't need to marinade meat that's processed (sausages and beefburgers).

Try out a few marinades beforehand to see which you prefer. A very easy one is detailed at the end of this chapter. Make your marinade and soak your meat in it for a few hours beforehand or in the fridge overnight, turning every hour or whenever you can. Chefs like to put their marinade in a big plastic bag with the meat, so they can really shake it up and move it around, allowing all the flavours to seep through.

Which marinade you choose is a matter of taste; just be careful if you're adding any strong spices that you don't let the meat marinade for too long. Also, any marinade recipe with sugar in it will burn very easily on the BBQ, so is best saved for food that can cook very quickly – like tiger prawns.

TIME-SAVING TIPS

Just because you have a gang of twenty arriving at 2 p.m., doesn't mean you have to get up at 5 a.m. to start preparing. Plan ahead and get most of the work done the day before. Here are some time-saving tips to take the stress out of BBQing for a crowd.

→ You can now buy supermarket meat ready-marinaded if you don't want to make your own. It costs more of course, but is handy if you're tight on time. Terry Farr, award-winning chef patron of Friends restaurant in Pinner, England, says, 'To me, a good barbecue is all about what goes with the meat. Simple marinades work well and you can get them ready beforehand. And make some dips or buy them ready-made from the supermarket, and put them into your own bowls.'

→ Cook your baked potatoes the day before. Tony Singh, head chef and co-founder of Scotland's Oloroso restaurant, says, 'Cook them plain, then rub them the next day with butter, garlic and herbs and put them on the BBQ to warm them through.'

→ Put meat under the grill for a few minutes until it's half-cooked. Finish it off on the BBQ for that lovely taste, without the wait. I always do this and it works a treat. Make sure it's piping hot before serving and never leave half-cooked meat lying around for ages as it allows bacteria to breed.

→ Make some food the day before, such as a large pasta salad or a bean salad, and place in the fridge. On the day, transfer to a pretty bowl and add dressing before serving.

→ Cook larger pieces of meat rather than kebabs. Threading skewers can be fiddly and time-consuming. Tony says, 'I go for whole king prawns, whole small fish, chicken breasts – food that doesn't need skewering. Otherwise you'll spend too long doing that and it spoils the fun of it all.'

→ There are several useful BBQ utensils you can buy that help you turn meat, or act as grilling tools. One looks like a flat square mesh grill on the end of a long handle. You lay the meat inside the grill, clamp it with a similar mesh grill on top to hold it in place, and use the handle to turn the whole thing easily. Particularly good for fiddly, delicate food like sardines. Use tongs, not forks, as prodding meat will allow juices to escape.

→ Prepare your plates, crockery, glasses and napkins beforehand. Use plastic picnic plates that you can wash and use again and again. Or paper ones if you prefer to avoid washing up. Avoid using china plates as they are heavy, a bit more cumbersome for guests, and something's bound to break. You can now get some very nice plastic 'glasses' that look like wine glasses or even plastic champagne flutes for picnics and BBQs. And, of course, you can wash them and use them again next time.

→ Set up a table either outdoors or just inside, to hold all the food and cutlery. Have a plastic tablecloth you can wipe, or a disposable paper one.

→ Get all your dishes and utensils out beforehand, as well as condiments and sauces.

ORGANISING YOUR SPACE OUTDOORS

→ Make sure you have enough chairs for the garden (especially if some of your guests are elderly), or failing that have a few blankets you can throw on the floor so people can lounge around. Although some people are happy to wander and nibble while they chat, many guests like to be able to sit down while they eat. Throw a few oversized cushions or beanbags on the grass to encourage people to relax. It's an informal event and people want to feel at home. (I once went to a BBQ where guests weren't allowed to stand on the lawn, because it had just been laid. Every time someone stepped on it, the host would come over and ask them to step off. Needless to say, the event never developed into a relaxed, lazy afternoon!)

→ Consider decorating your garden, especially if it's for a special event (e.g. a birthday) or is in the evening. If it's a BBQ to celebrate a family birthday, have a few balloons tied to bushes or hang streamers from a tree. In the evening, go to town with outdoor candles, lanterns and fairy lights, though do keep safety in mind. (For more advice on lighting outdoors, see Chapter 5.)

→ Is your garden or outdoor space safe for a BBQ? If you have children visiting, make sure any garden tools or equipment are out of the way.

→ Find a sheltered spot to set up your BBQ, so the wind isn't blowing the smoke into your guests/home. And keep it away from shrubs and trees, or anything flammable.

→ Buy some ice in bags from a supermarket or off-licence and use in a cold box for chilling drinks. Guests can help themselves throughout the event.

→ Have some bin liners to hand so that people can throw away debris as they go along. If you want to keep plastic plates, cutlery and glasses, let them know.

→ Have some sun block to hand for guests, especially children.

WHAT KIND OF BBQ TO BUY

Unless you're planning on throwing several BBQs a year, I'd advise against buying a permanent BBQ. They can take up a lot of space and often lie rusting at the end of the garden. However, if you fancy yourself as a bit of a BBQ wizard, then go ahead.

→ Have a practice run if you've never used this BBQ before. Try it out on a couple of friends. Also a great time to try out any new marinades you want to use.

→ Disposable BBQs are very good and easy to use. The pack will tell you how long you need to light the coals before you can use the BBQ. The general rule is that you have to let the flames die down and the coals turn white before trying to cook anything.

DRINK

Your BBQ will probably be held during the daytime, in the summer months. Chilled wine and ice-cold beer will of course go down well, but do make sure you have enough low- and non-alcoholic options, too. People tend to drink more in the heat, and the sun will also dehydrate everyone, so beware of running out of water, ice, juice and other soft drinks.

Most people don't like to drink a lot of alcohol during the day, they may also be driving, and children may be present so it's not appropriate for this to turn into a drunken affair. It's a great idea to make a non-alcoholic punch beforehand to serve as a welcome drink when guests arrive. Experiment with flavours, or try this: mix two bottles of 'homemade' lemonade mixed with cranberry juice and decorated with slices of lemon and orange. Put lots of crushed ice in the jug and serve it in long glasses to quench their thirst.

BBQ TIPS

→ Once cooked, allow the meat to 'rest' for a while (ten minutes is enough). During this time, the juices will return to the meat and it will feel wonderfully moist. Not necessary if cooking sausages, but do try to fend the hordes off for a few minutes if you're making steak or chops.

→ 'Don't leave cooked meat lying around,' says Charlotte Butterworth, party creator at Create Food (a bespoke catering company). 'To avoid salmonella, keep the oven on during the BBQ and use it to keep meat warm before it's served. Cover in foil to avoid it drying out, and don't leave for too long before serving.'

→ Chicken is done when the juices running from it are clear, with no sign of blood. It's *essential* you cook chicken right through to avoid food poisoning. If lamb or beef is left a bit rare, it doesn't matter.

→ If cooking a whole fish, oil the grill first and the fish itself. Make sure the BBQ is very hot, throw it on and leave it alone. It's ready once it comes away from the grill easily. You can get special utensils for grilling sardines.

→ Have a water spray on hand for damping down any flare-ups.

→ Don't ever leave your BBQ unattended, though do take shifts with a friend or any guest who offers to give you a break.

→ Have oven gloves to hand and wear an apron to protect from any fat or oil.

→ If your space is big enough, have a corner designated for children with games on hand (or ask their parents to bring along any toys they want). For safety, make the kids' area as far away from the BBQ as possible. If you're sitting people down to eat, set out a separate small table for the children, or a piece of plastic sheeting on the ground that's especially for them. (Don't try sitting toddlers at a table – they won't stay still.)

SOME MARINADE IDEAS

→ Yoghurt works well with chicken, as it helps tenderise the meat. Mix well with dried or fresh mint, place the chicken in it and leave for several hours in the fridge.

→ For red meat try this: olive oil, fresh rosemary, crushed garlic and lemon juice – vary amounts according to how much you're cooking. This marinade works wonderfully overnight (especially on lamb).

→ There are many supermarket marinades that you can add to your own meat – try a hickory-flavoured one on pork, or chilli on beef.

→ Mix maple syrup, balsamic vinegar and whole grain mustard together and add to chicken for a lovely sweet-sharp marinade.

FOR DESSERT

Tony says, 'Go for berries that are in season with flavoured double creams. Add a bit of kirsch, lime, lemon, mint, lemon grass – whatever you fancy. Try them out beforehand to get the proportions right.'

BBQ CRIB SHEET

→ Plan well and this needn't be exhausting. The day before, get as much of the work done as possible. Failing that, on the morning of the event.

→ If pushed for time buy ready-made salads (rather than boiling three pounds of potatoes at 7 a.m. to make that potato salad). Also go for ready-marinaded meat.

→ Remember to limit the variety of food. Guests will just choose what they like and it will save you a lot of work.

→ Don't run out of soft drinks or ice. (For more advice on drink, see Chapter 7.)

→ When working with a BBQ, make safety your priority.

→ Knackered and want them to leave? Give them dessert to send a message that the event is coming to an end. Keep it light – people are bound to be full. Piles of fresh berries with cream, or a handmade flan from a reputable bakery are ideal. Serve with tea or coffee to signify the end of the day.

16 A CHILDREN'S PARTY

As any parent can tell you, not only is there a growing trend towards children having parties to celebrate their birthdays, but there also seems to be a lot of pressure on parents these days to hold *the* best party ever, with the best entertainment and goody bags. This is peer pressure, all right, but it often comes from other parents as opposed to the children themselves. But rather than trying to impress other parents – there's always going to be someone who can organise a bigger, more expensive event than you, so what's the point? – try to throw a party your child will really love. Any child over the age of eight can help with ideas and organising the party. Within reason, listen to their requests. After all, whose party is this?

DON'T INVITE THE WHOLE CLASS

A kids' party is different to an adults' one, in that you should try to keep numbers as small as possible. At a grown-up party, if only four or five people turn up we see that as a sign of unpopularity. A party with a handful of children, however, is fine. Even though you may well want to throw the best, biggest party ever for your child, be practical.

The younger they are, the more room they and their friends are going to need to run around, and the more exhausting the whole thing will be for the host. You're going to be running around after them, keeping an eye on them. It's a good idea to enlist the help of another adult, to help with the party itself and in keeping things (fairly) under control. Many parents will happily drop off their children then return to pick them up, pleased to get an afternoon to themselves. But do make sure you have some kind of adult help at the party, and if you need someone to stay behind and help you, mention it beforehand. In fact, why not invite a couple of parents to stay and have some tea and cake with you while the party gets under way. After all, they're their children too and the last thing you want is half a dozen hyperactive five-year-olds running you ragged all afternoon.

Think about how many children you can handle in your house. Is it practical to have that many? Tell your child how many they're allowed to invite, and make sure you get definite RSVPs (otherwise invite someone else to make up numbers). Unless you have the patience of a saint and the stamina of an athlete, I'd recommend never going over six children for a party for under 13s. Also, keep the party restricted to a few hours, say between two o'clock and five is plenty of time. They'll all be exhausted by then and want to go home.

WHERE TO HOLD IT

Which room are you going to use? Choose somewhere the children can spread out and will be able to make a mess without you fretting over the new curtains or expensive furniture. If you have a playroom, or a conservatory, that could work well. Put breakables out of reach. If it's summer, get them out into the garden. Young children will not sit still so don't expect them to. Have some activities and games on hand that involve movement (see below).

Of course, you can always hold the party away from home. There are hundreds of places that host children's parties, from McDonalds to some that include activities, such as Colour Me Mine (where children sit and paint pottery). If you hire somewhere like this for a party it does, of course, push the cost up. One of the benefits, though, is you have to do very little work. Use your local directory to find venues for children's parties. For the purposes of this chapter, we're assuming the party is being held in your home.

WHAT KIND OF PARTY?

This really depends on the age of the child. Different children do have different needs, and (if you're the parent) you'll probably be quite clued up to what will work. See the quick guide below:

BABIES – 2 YEARS OLD

I question the point of throwing parties for very young children, as they really don't know what's going on, but often parents like to do this as a chance for them to get together with other parents. Make sure you invite three or four maximum, as the younger the children the more attention they'll need. Make sure the parents stay behind, too! A few balloons and decorations are enough to give it a festive feel, and ask parents what their children like to eat. Many will probably bring along some food anyway. Have lots of toys on hand, and try to keep it fairly low-key, otherwise you run the risk of exhausting the children and yourself. At this young age, booking an entertainer is a waste of money.

TODDLERS

This can be exhausting, so again keep numbers limited. If another child has a birthday around the same day, consider getting together with their parents and throwing a joint party. Have toys and games to hand for entertainment, but also expect the children to want to move around a lot. If your child has a favourite TV or film character, try some themed partyware (e.g. Bob the Builder, the Tweenies). Buying themed paper plates, napkins and balloons is an effective, cheap way to make a kids' party come alive. Again, booking an entertainer for this age group is not a good use of your money – wait until they're older.

BETWEEN 5 AND 7 YEARS OLD

This is the stage at which they become very active. If possible, let them have the party outdoors in the garden. Children need space to charge around, play and exert their incredible energy. Would you rather they did that in your just-decorated lounge or in your garden? Exactly. As well as toys, have some outdoor games, a football and skipping ropes to hand. Hiring an entertainer, such as a magician or a clown, can work well for this age group, but keep his/her performance short as their attention span is limited. (See below for details.)

BETWEEN 8 AND 13 YEARS OLD

At this age, your child can be involved in planning their party. Within reason, do listen to what they would like and the kind of entertainment they want. Don't assume you know; children's fads change remarkably quickly, so what's cool one week isn't necessarily so the next. Get them involved in choosing the food and the music, as they'll know better than you what their friends would appreciate.

'With children's parties you have to be very careful with the music,' says William Higham, a marketing and trends consultant who's worked in the music industry for fifteen years, for companies such as Sony, Virgin and Universal. 'It's easy to get it wrong so your best bet is to leave it up to them to choose what to play. You can have something a bit more mellow playing in another room for you and the other parents, because you're bound to get sick of S Club Juniors after a while!'

Let them have a certain amount of privacy and independence as they get older. They don't need to be constantly watched over, so let them get on with it while you have a drink with another couple of parents in the next room. (Don't at this age leave them home alone.) As they get older, girls in particular will probably want to go out with their friends instead of having a party at home. They may want to go for lunch at a local pizza restaurant, for example. Go along, but don't sit with them. You and a couple of other parents can sit at a separate table a little distance away.

TEENAGERS

Uh-oh. Are you *really* going to have a party in your house? Again, let them take part in organising it and be prepared to take a bit of a back seat. Obviously, you'll actually be expected to do the hard work, like any cooking, but to disappear once their friends arrive. Make sure they understand some basic ground rules – no smoking, keep out of the drinks cupboard, bedrooms are out of bounds – and you should be OK. Try to keep any parties to the daytime until they're a bit older.

A proper party may be considered uncool, so your teens may want to invite a few friends round to hang out or listen to music. (For more information on music at parties, see Chapter 8.) This is the age at which anything you do will embarrass them. Make sure they've got food on hand, then get out of their way. And whatever you do, don't hire that magician ...

HIRING AN ENTERTAINER

Entertainers for a younger children's party can be expensive, so make sure you get it right. Research local entertainers and ask friends and other parents for ones they recommend (or who to steer clear of). Entertainers can range from jugglers to clowns, musicians, magicians, storytellers – the list is endless. Here are some tips to getting what you want, but for in-depth information on hiring a professional, see Chapter 11.

→ The most important thing is making sure your entertainer is relevant for the age group. Check them out first. Either see them in action or watch a video of them performing. If they come on recommendation alone, make sure you trust the source.

→ Be specific about what you want and ask if they can provide it. Have they performed at many events like yours before? Ask to speak to other satisfied customers.

→ Does their charge include fares? How long will their performance last? What time will they start and finish?

→ What will they wear? Will they arrive 'in character' or will they need somewhere to get changed?

→ Give them as much information about the children coming, their ages, sexes, and any particular 'likes' that they can work into their performance (for example if the children are Britney fans, perhaps they can work her into one of the stories).

GAMES

There are several games that younger children like playing, and that are cheap and easy to organise. Try musical chairs, statues or pass the parcel. Playing games is a good way of getting them to focus on one thing while all being in one place. If you are playing games that involve winning presents, make sure there's enough to go around and, at the end of the game, give a gift to any child who didn't win one.

WHAT DO THEY EAT?

When catering for a children's party, always speak to parents first about any allergies the child may have. If any of the children have a nut allergy, ban all food containing nuts from the party. Many processed foods are made in factories that also make foods using nuts, so be careful. Food labels state if this is the case.

As a kid, remember when you used to just eat anything in sight? Today's growing health concerns mean that some parents are very particular about what they 'allow' their children to eat (for example, some don't like their children eating processed food, or drinking orange squash that has additives in it). You may think this is ridiculous, but you have to respect their wishes. However, find out if the parents are willing to be flexible for the duration of the party, as you'll probably be serving some food like this. If they're not, then ask them to stay at the party with you so they can monitor their child's food intake. The last thing you want is to have to 'police' a child when you're trying to throw a party.

MAKING LIFE EASIER

→ Don't try sitting toddlers at a table – they won't stay still. Place a disposable or wipe-clean tablecloth on the floor, put all the food on it, and the kids around. Make sure your plates and bowls are all disposable.

→ If they're older and you want to sit them at a table, interiors stylist, Carl Braganza says, 'Make an effort to decorate the table. It'll add to the sense of fun. Don't use a tablecloth. Put brightly-coloured crêpe paper runners along the table. You can add some packs of jellybeans for them to eat after the meal and maybe some indoor sparklers, too.'

→ To save on mess, put a selection of food into individual party boxes and hand one out to each child. That keeps everything self-contained and avoids them having to juggle plates of crisps and sandwiches. You can buy themed party boxes from all good party suppliers and some supermarkets (see Resources section at the end).

→ Have lots of wet wipes on hand to avoid having to wash a dozen dirty little faces.

→ Make sure you have some plasters to hand in case of accidents.

→ Take a phone number for each parent who's depositing their child. If they're going out, take their mobile number in case of emergencies.

→ If you're inviting a child and they have a sibling around the same age, invite them too, especially if your child knows them both.

FOOD IDEAS FOR A CHILDREN'S PARTY

Children are famous for being picky when it comes to food, and what you serve will very much depend on their age and personal likes and dislikes. You don't have to cater to every whim, but do have enough of a variety available so that those kids who suddenly declare that they don't like sandwiches don't go home hungry.

→ Have food that's easy to eat – remember your guests have tiny hands!
  Mini sandwiches, sausages and small chocolates are fun.
→ Have a good mix of savoury and sweet. Don't bring the sweet food out
  until you've had the savoury.
→ Tony Singh, head chef and co-founder of Scotland's top restaurant
  Oloroso, says, 'Make the food colourful, with different textures. If it looks
  interesting they'll probably eat anything. And do have some of the stuff
  they like, such as biscuits, jellies and cakes.'
→ If it's a birthday, have a cake. You can buy some great ready-made
  'character' cakes now from supermarkets, or order one from your local
  bakers and ask for the child's name to be iced on top. If you're a baking-
  cakes sort of person you can, of course, make your own. A friend of mine,
  who's always been football mad, has never forgotten his 12th birthday
  when his mum made him an amazing cake that looked like a football
  pitch, complete with green icing and tiny footballers.
→ Don't have lots of fizzy drinks – still drinks are better as kids don't fill up
  on them.
→ Don't make food you would like to eat – this party isn't for you. Keep
  sandwich fillings simple, such as ham, cheese, jam. Keep the gourmet
  fillings for a grown-up event.
→ Avoid food that has debris/bones/pips that need spitting out.
→ Unlike grown-ups, most kids just stop eating when they're full, so don't
  over cater. Nobody expects you to provide a proper meal at a children's
  party. Do make sure, however, that you have enough of the stuff that
  makes it a party – cake and crisps.

THEMING THE PARTY

Children love themes, and there are so many products available
that can help you decorate and theme your party at the same time
(see the Resources chapter at the end). Even if you decide not to
theme your party, make sure you spend some time decorating the
house as children enjoy sensory overload. You needn't spend much
money – get some balloons, streamers and paper hats.

→ Choose a theme that reflects the child's passions – if they're a football
  fan, and their friends are too, get them to wear their strips. Or maybe
  they love Harry Potter? Ask them to come as witches and wizards.
→ Children love dressing up, though try to choose a theme that is easy for
  parents to provide for.
→ Send out themed invitations to stir up some excitement beforehand.
→ Themes help narrow down your choices as a host. They may help you
  decide on decor, food, drink and music, making the event easier to host.

→ **As soon as a themed event starts being a chore you know you've either chosen the wrong theme or taken it too far.**

(For more on theming, see Chapter 4.)

GOODY BAGS

It's the norm at a children's party now to send off your young guests with a goody bag. This can be anything from a piece of cake wrapped up and a balloon to remember the party by, to something a lot more extravagant. There are companies who specialise in preparing goody bags, and can cater for any occasion. Maria Hipwell and Liz Ellerton are founders of Lilies and Chips, a company that makes bespoke goody bags and invitations. 'Kids love goody bags,' they say. 'Make them relevant to the ages of the children at the party. Sweets always go down well, as do some sort of small toy or game they can take to school the next day and show their friends in the playground. You can buy ready-made goody bags for children – so for Harry Potter, for example, you can get a bag stuffed with things related to the books. You can go and do it yourself, of course, but there are companies that do all the work for you.'

CHILDREN'S PARTY CRIB SHEET

→ Keep numbers limited. Don't underestimate how exhausting a houseful of five-year-olds can be.
→ Make sure you discuss any allergies with parents beforehand.
→ Have food that says 'party' rather than the kind of food you'd like to eat.
→ Use a theme to give a children's party a sense of occasion and fun.
→ Don't forget the goody bag. Even something simple like some sweets are better than nothing.
→ And remember – don't get caught up in trying to impress other parents. This party is for your child, not them.

17 A SUMMER PICNIC

Throwing a summer picnic will make you a very popular person – people love them. Whether it's the idea of being outdoors on a summer's day, the informality of lounging on the grass while you eat and drink, or the spontaneity of grabbing some food and making for the hills, picnics seem to get everyone's vote.

They're often arranged at the last minute, and, as you're not going to be sitting round a table, you can be more generous with your guest list, inviting as many people as you like. You'll be outdoors so space isn't an issue. Unlike dinner parties, you don't need to decide on a set menu. People will pick and choose to eat what they like. So as long as you have a good balance of savoury and sweet, with plenty of drinks, you'll be fine.

Hosting a picnic still needs thought and a bit of preparation but, frankly, if you find you're rushed off your feet and exhausted by the time everyone arrives then you're doing something wrong. Don't try to make this a dinner party outdoors – accept that it's a picnic and the food will be casual and easy to cook and eat. Your guests are bound to have a great time as there are few things in life as pleasurable as eating alfresco on a gorgeous summer's day.

As host, you too should have an easy time of it. A picnic is one of the easiest events to cater for. In fact, if you have little experience of entertaining, start off with a picnic. Here's how to make sure yours is a success.

WHO TO INVITE

Picnics seem to work well whatever the numbers. Perhaps you want to plan a romantic picnic for just you and your partner to celebrate a birthday or an anniversary. Maybe you're throwing a large family picnic, where the crowd descends, kids and all. Or you may have a few friends who've never met and you'd like to get them together. A picnic is a great opportunity to invite people who perhaps you'd be a bit reluctant to mix at a dinner party. For some reason, the relaxed atmosphere seems to work its magic and people just seem to be more sociable at picnics.

Most people expect to bring some food or drink along to a picnic, so do ask guests to contribute (especially if you're catering for a larger crowd). It's a good idea to tell them what you'd like them to bring. Perhaps they can be in charge of bringing fruit, or something sweet for dessert. If someone is contributing an essential component of your picnic food, do make sure they're reliable and that they're the sort of people who will turn up. If you've invited anyone who's likely to change their mind at the last minute, don't ask them to bring anything that's essential, in case they don't turn up.

Picnics for children can be a great success, especially if you theme them using, for example, Disney character plates and napkins. For ideas on children's parties, see Chapter 16.

WHEN TO INVITE

The very nature of picnics means they tend to be spontaneous affairs. You may call friends and plan yours just the day before, or even on the day itself. As with all aspects of entertaining, the more time you have, the less work there will be to do on the day, as you can get your preparation done well in advance. But the way it usually works is that you hear a weather report that predicts a heat wave and you decide to make the most of it. There's not enough spontaneity in life – so go with it. The great thing about picnics is that numbers don't matter; whether you end up with two of you or twenty, it's still a picnic.

If you want the food at your picnic to be special (perhaps you're celebrating something) then of course you're advised to plan ahead. You'll need the extra time to prepare and cook, or order from your local deli.

FINDING THE PERFECT SPOT

The last thing you want to do on the day is trudge around trying to find that perfect spot. Think about the location beforehand and, if possible, pop down to check it out. At the height of summer even the most peaceful spots can get crowded. That may not be a problem if there's a crowd of you going, but if you're aiming for a romantic picnic you probably don't want to be surrounded by a dozen toddlers playing with water pistols.

WHAT TO CONSIDER

→ Are there toilets and washing facilities nearby? Essential if you're going to be there any length of time, particularly if you have children coming along.

→ Are you sitting near water? Will there be mossies? Take some repellent.

→ Is there shade nearby? If not, consider taking a garden umbrella if you're travelling by car. A good spot is often under a tree where those who are sun worshippers can lie out and everyone else can take cover. Remember the sunblock, even if it's a cloudy day.

→ Is it a picnic area with tables and benches provided? Useful if you're inviting anyone elderly, who may find sitting on the grass uncomfortable.

→ Is there shelter somewhere nearby if it rains?

→ Are you allowed to picnic here? There will be signs if you can't.

IDEAS FOR LOCATIONS

You can picnic in all kinds of places, though do look out for any signs telling you otherwise, leave the area as you found it, and take your litter with you. The most important considerations are that you have a nice view and it's easy for your guests to get to. Here are some ideas:

→ A local park with grass

→ A stately home with beautiful grounds and gardens (you can combine it with a day out, and most of these places have specified picnic areas with good facilities)

→ The beach

→ Your roof-terrace or garden (handy if you forget something)

→ A forest

→ By a lake or river

→ At an outdoor evening concert (such as Kenwood, in North London). Many cities offer free summer concerts, where you can go along with a picnic, listen to the music and watch fireworks at the end of the evening. See your local listings for details. If you're having an evening picnic, take some layers as it's bound to get chilly when the sun goes down.

→ If children are invited, choose a space that's open and away from water, where you'll be able to keep an eye on them at all times.

FOOD FOR A PICNIC

There are just two points to consider when packing your picnic:

1. Will this food keep for several hours and still taste good?

2. Is it easy to transport?

Then it really is up to you. Some people like a bit of luxury when it comes to picnics, taking along cold champagne, strawberries, mini tartlets and the kind of canapés you might find at a smart drinks party. You may want to have this style of picnic, particularly if you are celebrating a special event. If so, check out your local deli or gourmet food store, as they often cater for upmarket picnics and can save you a lot of cooking time. Or, if money's no object, you may want to get a hamper that's ready-prepared. See the Resources section at the end of the book for details.

At a picnic, it really is OK to buy food ready-prepared – the informality means nobody expects you to have slaved over a hot stove for days on end. There's definitely a trend towards luxury picnics, and they're particularly good if you're eating in the evening at an outdoor summer concert.

If you'd rather have something less formal, go for food that's a bit rough and ready, more substantial, and that people can eat with their hands, such as fried chicken drumsticks, crudités and dips, and mini-samosas and mini-sausages. Charlotte Butterworth, party creator at Create Food (a bespoke catering company) says, 'Go for food that's tasty and not too delicate. It'll be easier to transport.'

WON'T A PILE OF SANDWICHES DO?

No. If your idea of picnic food is a heap of sandwiches you prepared that morning, think again. Sandwiches are fine as a component of what you offer, but don't make them the main attraction, otherwise it will be a very boring picnic. Think about small pizzas, salami, roasted veg, cheese, crackers, potato salad, pasta salad, green salad (take the dressing along separately in a screw-lid jar, and add at the last minute). The list is endless. The only items I'd avoid are anything that's very fiddly to eat, or won't withstand a few hours out of the fridge (such as salmon or eggs).

HOW TO MAKE YOUR SANDWICHES SPECIAL

As soon as you decide you're having a picnic, it's hard to fight the impulse to start buttering loaves of bread and filling them with your favourite combinations. Tony Singh, head chef and co-founder of Scotland's top restaurant Oloroso, says, 'Never make sandwiches for a picnic. By the time you get them there they'll get soggy. Just butter the bread beforehand and take along a variety of fillings. Everybody can then make up their own sandwiches and they will be able to choose from endless variations. It'll save you work, too.'

Also, think about using unusual breads, rather than just your standard white sliced, such as focaccia, ciabatta, raisin bread, pitta or walnut bread. People love experimenting with flavours and being able to customise their sandwiches.

DRINK

Anything goes at a picnic, but keep in mind that you may be sitting in the sun for a few hours, so excessive alcohol probably isn't a good idea. By all means take a bottle or two of cold wine, but also take lots of water and soft drinks. Keep all your drink in the fridge until just before you leave, then transfer to an insulated cold box. If you don't have one, double wrap bottles in newspaper and they'll stay cold for a while. Small bottles (of beer, water, soft drinks) are preferable to large ones. They're easier to transport and pour and stay colder for longer. And don't forget the corkscrew!

WHAT ABOUT PLATES?

Please don't take plates that break – they will. There are lots of pretty plastic picnic plates on the market, along with cutlery, and it's all reusable. Failing that, use paper plates that you can discard later.

REMEMBER TO PACK . . .

Not all of this is essential but it will probably make life easier.

→ A blanket/cloth for sitting on. Make sure it isn't itchy.

→ A disposable paper tablecloth to lay on the ground and place food on, or wipe-clean plastic sheeting you can use again

→ Plates, knives, forks, corkscrew.

→ Glasses/cups – either reusable plastic ones or throwaway.

→ Any games/toys for younger guests.

→ A radio or portable tape recorder with some favourite music.

→ Salt and pepper.

→ Mossie repellent or citronella candles if you're out at night. Charlotte says, 'Consider taking some hurricane lanterns or tea lights along.'

→ Sun cream if you're out during the day.

→ Paper napkins.

→ Cushions (particularly appreciated by people who aren't outdoor types).

→ Bin liners for your debris which, of course, you'll dispose of responsibly!

HOW TO AVOID FOOD POISONING

It's vital you stick to a few simple rules to avoid giving your guests a nasty bout of food poisoning.

→ A cold box is a good investment and isn't just for picnics. It's a useful item if you have a small fridge and entertain a lot, as you can use it to keep drink cold at a party when you run out of space (and beats having to go to the bathroom to get drink out of the bath every time you run out). If you're having a large picnic, you may want two cold boxes – one for drink and another for food – otherwise you'll be opening it constantly and the temperature inside will rise. When you get to your picnic site, put your cold box and any food as much in the shade as possible.

→ Keep cold food cold: if food is meant to be cold (such as potato salad or sandwich fillings) then keep it in your fridge until the last minute. Then put into a cold box if possible, or find a picnic spot near home so your food won't be sitting in a car for hours before you eat it. On a summer's day, it is easy for cold food to warm up quickly, so don't risk letting bacteria breed.

→ And keep hot food hot: if you really want to serve something hot (like fried chicken, for example) make sure you wrap it in foil to keep in the heat. You can buy thermal containers that help keep food hot. Personally, I'd avoid serving anything hot at a picnic as I think it just causes headaches. Cook any meat you want to serve several hours beforehand, refrigerate once cooled, then transfer to a cool box for transporting.

→ Take along some anti-bacterial hand/face wipes.

→ Once it's over, throw away any food that's perishable (i.e. anything that would normally be kept in the fridge such as meat, food with egg in it, cheese, etc.). Fruit is fine to keep.

PACKING IT ALL IN

Keep the following in mind when packing your food:

→ Don't use heavy containers for your food. You'll have to bring them home, so choose light, plastic ones, or wrap food in foil.

→ Place heavy items at the bottom; lighter, more delicate ones on the top.

→ If you're taking along any salad dressing/other liquid, put it in a screw-top jar then place in a sealed plastic bag. Assume leakable things will leak!

→ If you don't have a cold box, wrap any bottles /other breakables in blankets, cardigans, whatever else you're taking along.

SUMMER PICNIC CRIB SHEET

→ Relax – this isn't a dinner party. Informality rules at picnics.

→ The 'perfect spot' for a picnic is somewhere that's safe, clean and pretty. Don't become obsessive about finding somewhere idyllic.

→ It's easy to get food poisoning if you're careless. See the rules above for a foolproof guide.

→ Supply a good variety of food, remembering to cater for veggies and anyone with special requirements. Don't just think 'sandwiches'.

→ Ask guests to contribute and get an idea of what they're bringing.

→ Don't drag along real plates, knives and forks. You're on a picnic, not sitting outdoors at a restaurant. Make the most of the picnicware now available, that you can wash and reuse.

18 PLANNING A WEDDING RECEPTION

Weddings are very special. They are, hopefully, once-in-a-lifetime occasions. Planning a wedding reception will probably be the biggest, most formal, most expensive and possibly stressful event you'll ever have to handle. But it needn't be a nightmare. In fact, if you leave enough time and are clear and realistic about what you can afford, the sense of anticipation can make it great fun. However, if you start planning something swish at the last minute, on a zero budget, you'll probably have a breakdown.

This chapter shows you how to plan a reception using a simple step-by-step checklist, explaining what should be done, when. For simplicity's sake, I'm assuming you're one half of the happy couple – if not, you'll obviously need to communicate well with the couple as to the style of wedding they want and how much control they're willing to hand over to you. This chapter focuses on the wedding reception itself. It doesn't cover the legal requirements for getting married, service, bridesmaids, sorting out your honeymoon, and so on. It's simply about the party. There's plenty of advice around for these other areas (see the Resources chapter at the end for some excellent online wedding planners).

HOW MUCH?

We may as well tackle this one early as you'll have to come back to it again and again when making decisions. It is *vital* you have a budget for your wedding. Even if you're a laid-back sort of person who usually doesn't bother with this kind of thing, you simply *cannot* afford to ignore costs. It's very easy to spend too much. Along every step of the way, you'll be faced with decisions to make: what kind of flowers? what sort of food? what drink? Make these decisions easier by knowing what you can afford. I'm not suggesting you write up a spreadsheet, but do at least make a list of every item you need to pay for with prices quoted for certain services by the side. Before confirming your florist, caterer, etc., add it up and get a picture of the total cost. Then you can see where you may be able to cut back. Chapter 3 looks at budgets in detail.

WHAT TO CONSIDER

→ Decide on how much you can afford to spend (and want to spend). What are your personal wedding priorities? A fantastic disco? An idyllic honeymoon? Sitting a hundred people down to a sumptuous three-course meal? Make your priorities the area where you spend most of your money.

→ Decide on the kind of wedding you want. Do you want something very smart and big? Kitsch and fun? Informal for close friends only? How many guests would you like to invite? The style of wedding you choose, where you want to hold it, and the numbers invited will have a great influence on your final bill.

→ Do some research. Check out various venues and professionals offering services, and get price estimates for the numbers you want to invite. Do you need to rethink the kind of wedding you're having or the numbers invited?

→ Plan ahead. Some couples start with over a year in hand (though, as long as you've booked your ceremony I think you can comfortably plan most weddings about 6–8 months ahead). The later you leave it, the less choice you'll have and more expensive it can turn out. If anyone provides a service for you faster than they normally would, they will charge you more than the going rate. As you'll have left it late, you will have little choice but to pay. Also, any half-decent professionals will be booked up for several weeks ahead.

SO WHAT DO I HAVE TO PAY FOR?

Remember, this is only a list for the reception. Your honeymoon, outfits, bridesmaids outfits, ceremony charges, rings and so on will have to be added to this. This isn't a definitive list, it's a starting point. Customise it according to your needs.

Invitations and postage

Venue hire

Car to get you to venue

Decorations at venue (e.g. candles, fairy lights, disco lights, table dressings)

Flowers (for venue, tables, buttonholes and bouquet)

Food for guests

Drink for guests, including champagne for toast

Hire of glasses, crockery, tables, chairs, and any other equipment

Photographer/video recorder

Caterer

Serving/waiting staff

Bar staff

DJ/music/band

Late licence (should you want your party to go on later than is allowed, speak to the banqueting/venue manager)

A party planner/organiser: if you're feeling flush, you may want to hire one of these. They can look after the whole event for you. Good if you have a healthy budget, not so good if you're a control freak. Costs can be high and vary greatly, but they have the power to negotiate better deals for you with known suppliers.

Coat check/meet and greet staff: the first people your guests will see. Can show guests to tables and give general information on venue's facilities, such as the toilets or telephones.

Cleaning staff: relatives often do this, but you may want to pay someone to take down any decorations and get the venue back in order once the event is over.

WHY BOTHER TO CALL IN THE PROFESSIONALS?

If you throw a birthday party and the DJ lets you down, or the food is awful, it's not the end of the world. People are pretty forgiving and, well, there's always next year. At a wedding, you don't get any second chances. If something goes wrong it will be remembered for years to come, by your guests as well as you.

You don't have to hire an expert for every aspect of your wedding, but you should for the ones you consider the most important. These people do this for a living, day in, day out, year after year. Make the most of their expertise. If you want to use a friend to play

DJ or take photos, that's fine. Just make sure they're up to it, know what you want and you can trust them to get it right. It's a big responsibility and one that only the confident and capable should take on.

TIPS ON HIRING PROFESSIONALS

There are many experts offering all kinds of services out there. From invitation-makers to interior designers for your venue, if you've got the money there's a person out there to provide the service. Chapter 11 looks at hiring professionals in detail, and I'd recommend you read it before you start planning your wedding. It explains what to look out for and how to get exactly what you want.

BASIC RULES

→ Allow as much time as possible so you can compare prices and sample services before making a final choice.

→ Communicate well with all the experts you're hiring. Show them what you want (take pictures along if necessary or examples) and ask to see their work. A good professional should be used to this kind of request. If it's a band you're hiring, watch a video of them at work or get them to come and do a dummy performance for you. A florist can show you examples of work. A chef/caterer should always offer you a tasting. 'You should really demand one,' says Charlotte Butterworth, party creator at Create Food (a bespoke catering company). 'This is one of the most important days of your life and you want to be happy with the food.'

→ Make sure you choose the right person for the right job. Weddings are unique occasions – a photographer may have lots of studio experience but be clueless about arranging groups of people for wedding photos. Make sure their experience is relevant.

→ Ask for and check out references yourself.

→ Get everything in writing, including a contract and prices.

→ Be open to their ideas, but don't let them side-track you into paying for something you don't want. If it's an autumn wedding and you've got your heart set on hot food, don't be bulldozed into accepting a cold buffet, simply because they'll find it easier. If they seem reluctant to provide what you want, go elsewhere.

→ That said, do listen to any advice they offer or any warnings that what you're trying to do is going to be very expensive or difficult to achieve. Ask them to suggest alternatives.

YOUR WEDDING TIMETABLE

When planning a wedding reception, there are certain things that need to be done in a certain order. Visit any of the wedding websites (listed in the Resources section) and you'll find that this list is fairly similar on all of them. Of course, it's flexible but do try to err on the side of caution. And do make sure you do things in this order – don't tell everyone the date, for example, before you've found a venue. How will you know you'll be able to invite them all? What if you can't find a venue big enough that you like, and you need to cut down on numbers?

'For a wedding the three rules are plan, plan, plan,' says Charlotte. 'Work out who is doing what and delegate. This will leave you free to enjoy your big day.'

On a final note, I have heard of couples who plan their weddings two years in advance. I don't know anyone who is that organised and, unless you desperately want a specific venue that's very popular, I really can't see the need for doing this. A year is plenty. I confess I did mine from beginning to end in about five months, but I wouldn't recommend it. It was stressful and, frankly, we were pretty lucky that we pulled it off.

8–12 MONTHS BEFORE

Set a date

Set a budget

Write out a rough guest list

Decide on your theme/style

What are your 'wedding priorities'?

Organise your ceremony/legal requirements

Start researching the following:

Venues

Photographer/video recorder

Caterer

DJ/band/musician

Florist

Cake

6 MONTHS BEFORE

Update your guest list

Shop for invitations (or look into getting them made)

Confirm your:

Venue

Photographer/video recorder

Caterer

DJ/band/musician

Florist

Cake

Book a car to get you to the reception after the ceremony

Plan a wedding day timetable, showing what happens, when. Make sure all your hired professionals have a copy, as well as family and friends helping out

Buy any rings

Start looking for outfits

3 MONTHS BEFORE

Send out your invitations

Buy outfits

Think about your seating plan. Lizz Clarke, a Dale Carnegie trainer who helps companies teach their staff how to network, says, 'This is the hardest part. Consider people's ages, what they do and personalities. Make yourself aware of any difficult relationships and keep these people apart. Parents and children need to be together. Place a special children's table near the adults' table.'

1 MONTH BEFORE

Agree on any final details with all your hired professionals

Ask your caterer for a tasting

FOOD AND DRINK

→ Deciding what food to serve at a wedding can be difficult, as you're trying to please so many people, often of varying ages and tastes. Terry Farr, award-winning chef patron of Friends restaurant in Pinner, England, recommends choosing a menu with broad appeal. 'For example, if you've got a hundred people don't serve calves' liver and bacon,' he says, 'as there will be several people who won't eat it. Avoid offal and shellfish. Chicken breast is always popular, as is salmon. Obviously, you need to cater for vegetarians, and anyone with allergies or special diets.'

→ You may want to theme your wedding meal. If it's high summer, you can offer a sunny, Mediterranean menu of roasted vegetables and couscous, for example. Or perhaps you want finger food that's a scaled down version of delicious meals, like duck wrapped in mini pancakes, and baby new potatoes with sour cream and bacon filling. If you'd like to try something a bit different from the usual 'chicken and two veg', speak to your caterer for inspiration. A good caterer will discuss the guests attending so s/he can decide on the best kind of menu.

→ Caterers can also advise on the amount of alcohol needed. Do use wine merchants who offer a drink or return deal, as they are by far the cheapest way to offer drink to a crowd.

→ If your venue is a hotel, they may want you to buy the wine from them, otherwise they'll charge corkage. Get all these details ironed out in your initial discussions before you confirm a booking. (For more information on what to ask when hiring a venue, see Chapter 11.)

WEDDING RECEPTION CRIB SHEET

→ Time is your enemy – make it your friend, by allowing at least six months before the big day.

→ Think about the style of wedding you want, how formal you'd like it to be and how much you can afford.

→ Think about the kind of decor you'd like. For some ideas on flowers, lights and place settings, see Chapter 5.

→ Start researching any professional help early. Talk to at least three people for each service you require, to give you a cost comparison. (Cheaper isn't always better – so check out their standard of work before you commit.)

→ Make a wedding timetable, detailing everything you need to do by when (see above). Divide the tasks between the two of you so one person doesn't feel pressurised into organising the whole thing. You can't start quarrelling yet – you're not even married.

→ Your wedding plans aren't set in stone – constantly review them every few weeks to make sure they're realistic, not costing too much and are what you really want. It's easy to get carried away when planning a wedding reception and end up with something that doesn't reflect your taste or style.

→ Lizz says, 'Make your own decisions and don't be influenced by those who think they know better.' Everyone (especially parents and close friends) will suddenly want to talk about the best way to plan a wedding/the flowers you should have/your venue, and so on. Smile pleasantly, nod enthusiastically, and do your own thing.

RESOURCES

This section is designed to provide a list of useful contacts when planning your events. These are the people who can make the whole thing happen. Check them out for yourself, compare prices and services with competitors and make sure you read Chapter 11, which gives some solid advice on how to go about hiring professionals.

CATERERS AND PARTY PLANNERS

www.createfood.co.uk

020 8870 1717

A leading bespoke catering and party design company that offers a stylish, modern take on entertaining. Can organise everything from lights, sound, design and catering.

CATERING EQUIPMENT HIRE

www.rayners.co.uk

020 8870 6000

Everything is for hire, from sparkling glasses to stylish furniture – all delivered to your venue. Prestigious company that's been in business for over seventy years. Can provide for any event, from a huge banquet to a dinner party in your own home.

CHILDREN'S PARTIES

www.kidspartyworld.com

American site specifically for kids' parties. Outfits, hats, balloons – you name it, it's here.

CLEANING

www.howtocleananything.com

A very useful site put together by a group of cleaners. Tips on cleaning just about anything – great if your party was a bit on the unruly side.

COOKING LESSONS

There are now hundreds of cookery courses available both here and abroad, and you can even go on cooking holidays to brush up on your culinary skills.

www.booksforcooks.com

020 7221 1992

Books for Cooks in London organise various workshops that specifically focus on party/finger food.

DECOR

www.general-trading.co.uk

The General Trading Company

020 7730 0411

2 Symons Street, Sloane Square, London SW3 2TJ

Recently voted the World's Best Home Design Shop by Forbes.com, this store provides a good source of inspiration for decorating your home.

FOOD IDEAS

www.allrecipes.com

Lots of ideas if you're stumped for what to serve.

FLOWERS AND CANDLES

www.kenturnerflowerschool.com

Kenneth Turner is one of the most innovative and influential floral decorators around, and his arrangements are available in both the UK and USA.

UK: 8 Avery Row, London W1K 4AL (020 7355 3880)

USA: 1 800 405 6841 (freephone)

www.floristpages.co.uk

Run by publishers of the UK's leading florist trade magazine, this site gives good tips on trends and buying the right flowers for the right occasion.

GAMES

www.giantindoorgames.com

Giant versions of nostalgia games – Twister, Operation, Jenga, Ker-plunk – available for party hire. Great for grown-ups as well as children.

GETTING THEM HOME

This idea has really caught on, so look in your local directory to find a similar service near you.

www.scooterman.co.uk

0870 242 6999

Ingenious. They arrive on a fold-up moped and drive any tipsy guests home in their own car.

www.onefortheroad.uk.com

020 7924 4141

For members only, but worth checking out as they offer a variety of services including taking guests home after a few drinks, as above.

INVITATIONS

www.liliesandchips.co.uk

020 7229 1002

16 Lambton Place, London, W11 2SH

Lilies and Chips is an innovative company that provides stylish, bespoke invitations, gifts, cards, party themes and paraphernalia.

LIGHTING

www.nomadirect.co.uk

Excellent site with lots of good, sound advice on lighting any event. Also sell practically everything you could need for lighting any party, however big or small.

MUSIC

www.cd-wow.com

The cheapest site around for CDs.

PARTY PLANNING AND THEMES

www.drparty.com

0870 900 0414

Owned by Sir Bob Geldof, Dr Party specialises in fabulous themed parties for private and corporate clients. Have a look at the great pictures from previous events on their website.

PICNICS (READY-MADE)

www.prezzybox.com

This manufacturer sells filled hampers for all kinds of celebrations. Good for special occasions as they include glassware, crockery, cutlery and even linen napkins.

www.netique.com/giftsearch/picnic.html

An American site doing much the same

www.sosgiftbaskets.com.au/

An Australian site for gift baskets, flowers and gourmet hampers for all occasions. Delivers across Australia and worldwide.

THEMES

www.partybox.co.uk

Packed with party supplies for all kinds of occasions, you can find tableware, wigs, goody bags, balloons and character merchandise, such as Harry Potter and Thomas the Tank Engine, for children's parties. Also provide tableware in colour themes.

www.partyplansplus.com

Very good, if slightly mad, American website with some excellent theming ideas and general information on planning any party.

www.partyproductsdirect.co.uk

Good range of themed products, but not just for kids. Includes colour themes for adult parties, too, such as silver napkins for anniversaries, etc.

www.thepartystore.co.uk

Extensive website worth a look. Particularly good for children's parties.

VENUE FINDER

www.Perfectvenue.com

Save time on finding your venue, this site has a database of over 400 venues for hire throughout the UK, many of them privately owned.

WEDDINGS

www.confetti.co.uk/

Lots of expert information and advice on planning everything from the legal requirements to the honeymoon. Also includes some useful online planning tools, so you can keep track of your progress as the big day approaches. Plus, a good range of UK wedding suppliers.

www.topweddinglinks.com

An American wedding planning site. Slightly traditional but still useful.

www.topweddinglinks.com/NationalDirectory/au/

Wedding advice and information for Australia.

WINE

www.bbr.com

0870 900 4300

Berry Bros & Rudd are prestigious, authoritative wine merchants with a very useful website which includes rules on food matching, plus tips on buying wine. They even hold wine tastings. Great if you want to learn more or just need to know where to start.

www.majestic.co.uk

The UK's biggest (and best) mixed-case wine retailer. Order online with free delivery, or visit a store where the staff are incredibly patient and helpful. Invaluable if you're buying wine for a large event, like a wedding.

www.virginwines.com

Offers a good selection of mixed cases and will replace your case if it's stolen from your front door.

www.wineontheweb.com

An American wine magazine online, which offers good consumer advice including tips on buying wine.

www.winesofnz.com

Wines of New Zealand

A useful site that celebrates, yes, wines of New Zealand.

www.australianwines.com.au

Information on Australian wines, with regional maps and tips on knowing what's what.

ACKNOWLEDGEMENTS

I'd like to thank the following people for their time and expert help in putting together this book: Fiona Sims, Lizz Clarke, William Higham, Tony Singh of Oloroso, Terry Farr of Friends, Danielle Nay at Dr Party, Carl Braganza at *You* magazine, Maria Hipwell and Liz Ellerton of Lilies and Chips and Pam Carter from the Savoy. Plus my friends Rosalind Lowe (for her excellent contacts) and Nicole Carmichael (for her cleaning-up-the-morning-after advice).

INDEX